Praise for
JUDGE AND JURY

"In **Judge and Jury**, *Helland and Tabarrok provide a superb and pioneering examination of the litigation nightmare in the United States. This book is indispensable reading on how to solve this enormous problem.*"
—**Paul H. Rubin**, Samuel Candler Dobbs Professor of Economics and Law, Emory University

"**Judge and Jury** *helps us understand how the legal system has been perverted to enrich some litigators at the expense of everyone in our society. The belief that we can live in a zero-risk society would mean a return to the stone age. As with any part of our legal system, when the jury system goes astray from its intended purpose, and juries begin to make social statements with their massive verdicts, reform is necessary. Helland and Tabarrok provide analytical guidance as to the reasons for the tort law problem in America, the size of it, and how meaningful reform can protect the rights of those who have suffered real injuries.*"
—**Roger E. Meiners**, Goolsby Distinguished Professor of Economics and Law, University of Texas, Arlington

"*Anyone who wants to know what's happened to American tort law in the last thirty years needs to read* **Judge and Jury**. *Helland and Tabarrok have written the definitive account of the evolution of tort law in the United States, using data rather than anecdotes. This superb book sets out a persuasive, interest-group-based account of the changes in U.S. tort law in the last half century. If data makes your heart beat faster, as it does mine, this is the book to read, and every legislator should do so.*"
—**Andrew P. Morriss**, Galen J. Roush Professor of Business Law & Regulation, Case Western Reserve University

"*Clear, forcefully argued and highly accessible,* **Judge and Jury** *makes the perfect introduction to the work of two of today's most provocative and talked-about empirical legal scholars.*"
—**Walter K. Olson**, author, *The Rule of Lawyers* and *The Litigation Explosion*; Senior Fellow, Manhattan Institute

"*Eric Helland and Alexander Tabarrok are doing essential and provocative empirical work on the critical public policy issue of the American litigation system....* **Judge and Jury** *is required reading for anyone who wishes to debate the need for civil justice reform.*"
—**Theodore Frank**, Resident Fellow and Director, Liability Project, American Enterprise Institute

Judge and Jury

Judge and Jury
American Tort Law on Trial

Eric Helland and Alexander Tabarrok

The INDEPENDENT INSTITUTE

Oakland, California

The Independent Institute
100 Swan Way, Oakland, CA 94621-1428
Telephone: 510-632-1366 · Fax: 510-568-6040
Email: info@independent.org
Website: www.independent.org

Library of Congress Cataloging-in-Publication Data

Helland, Eric.
    Judge and jury : American tort law on trial /
    Eric Helland and Alexander Tabarrok.
        p. cm.
    Includes bibliographical references and index.

    ISBN-13: 978-0-945999-99-7 (alk. paper)
    ISBN-10: 0-945999-99-2 (alk. paper)

    1. Torts–United States. 2. Judicial process–United States.
3. Law reform–United States. I. Tabarrok, Alexander. II. Title.
    KF1251.H45   2005
    346.7303–dc22

                                                            2005025815

10 9 8 7 6 5 4 3 2 1   06 07 08 09 10

Contents

Acknowledgments

Judge and Jury: American Tort Law on Trial draws from our academic work published over a number of years. We thank the following publishers for the right to draw from this material: The University of Chicago Press for "Race, Poverty, and American Tort Awards: Evidence from Three Datasets," *Journal of Legal Studies* (2003) 32: 27–58; Oxford Journals for "Runaway Judges? Selection Effects and the Jury," *Journal of Law, Economics, and Organization* (2003) 16 (2): 306–333; "Contingency Fees, Settlement Delay and Low-Quality Litigation: Empirical Evidence from Two Datasets," *Journal of Law, Economics, and Organization* (2003) 19 (2): 517–542; and "The Effect of Electoral Institutions on Tort Awards," *American Law and Economics Review* (2002) 4 (2): 341–370; The American Enterprise Institute for *Two Cheers for Contingent Fees*, Washington, D.C.: AEI Press, 2005.

1

Introduction

Recently, each of us has successfully sued more than half a dozen large corporations. No, we are not outrageously rich plaintiffs' lawyers or the attorney general of New York. In fact, neither of us even knew we were a party to these suits until we received letters telling us that a lawyer had sued on our behalf. Like millions of Americans, we discovered, after the fact, in a mass mailing, that we were part of class-action suits resulting in settlements. Among our winnings was a $5 coupon from Microsoft. "Our" lawyers must have done a good job: They will receive $112.4 million.[1]

It's cases like these that first interested us in the tort system. As empirical researchers trained in economics, however, we prefer data to anecdote. The media thrives on memorable anecdotes. Who has not heard of the lady who successfully sued McDonald's after she spilled hot coffee on herself?[2] But who can say what the average award is in a product liability suit? Or what has happened to awards, filings, and settlements over time?

In our investigations of the tort system we heard many fascinating anecdotes from lawyers. We heard about the "Bronx effect," a term coined by Tom Wolfe, who in his novel *The Bonfire of the Vanities* describes a plaintiff's lawyer who files malpractice claims in the poor, minority-dominated community of the Bronx because "The Bronx jury is a vehicle for redistributing the wealth." We also heard how plaintiffs' lawyers biased elected judges with campaign contributions and about how contingency fees were encouraging frivolous lawsuits and driving awards skyward. But no one really knew whether these anecdotes, even if true, happened often enough to warrant concern.

In this book, we present some data on the tort system, and we put some of the most interesting anecdotes to the test. As you will see, some of the anecdotes hold water, but others turned out to be all wet. We begin with an overview of the expansion of the U.S. tort system over the past thirty years.

THE EXPANSION OF THE TORT SYSTEM

Newsweek referred to a "litigation explosion" in its December 15, 2003, front-page story, "Lawsuit Hell." Is there a litigation explosion? Not everyone agrees. Public Citizen, the nonprofit advocacy group founded by Ralph Nader, accused *Newsweek* of gross distortions:

> *Newsweek* has fallen hook, line and sinker for the myths and distortions spread by a well organized campaign funded by the American Medical Association, insurers, tobacco companies, auto manufacturers and others to strip consumers —but, notably, not businesses—of their legal rights. Since big business dominates the political system, the civil justice system is the one branch of government in which ordinary citizens can hope to get a fair shake. That's why these entities are hell-bent on slamming the courthouse door shut.[3]

What do the data say? The longest chronological evidence on the growth in the U.S. tort system comes from Tillinghast-Towers Perrin (2000), a private consulting firm. Tillinghast's estimate is based on insurance industry data and includes the legal costs of defending policy-holders, the benefits paid to policy-holders' victims, the administrative cost of the insurance policies, and estimates of other costs associated with the tort system but not paid directly by insurance companies.[4] By Tillinghast's measure, expenditures in the tort system have increased greatly in the last thirty years, tripling in real terms from 1970 to 2001.

Even measured against GDP, the increase in tort expenditures is significant. Figure 1 shows tort expenditures as a percentage of GDP since 1970. From just over 1 percent of GDP in the early 1970s, tort costs nearly doubled to more than 2 percent of GDP in the late 1980s. In the late 1980s and early 1990s, Florida, California, and other states began to pass tort reform laws capping punitive damages and pain-and-suffering awards, modifying joint and several liability rules, restricting contingency fees, limiting who can be sued, and so forth (CBO 2004).[5] Tort expenditures as a fraction of GDP began to decline in the 1990s, probably as a result of these reforms.

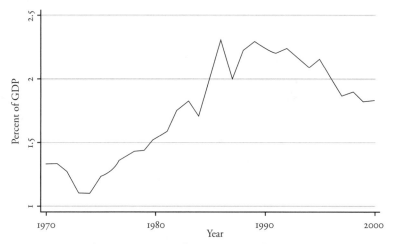

FIGURE 1 Tort Expenditures as a Percent of GDP. Source: Tillinghast-Towers Perrin, U.S. Tort Costs: 2003 Update, Trends and Findings on the Costs of the U.S. Tort System, 2003.

A more direct measure of the growth in the tort system can be found by examining trial awards. Figure 2 graphs the mean trial award (winning cases only) by year from two of the longest datasets on tort awards, the Administrative Office of the U.S. Courts data (hereafter the Federal data) and a series put together by researchers at the RAND Corporation drawing from state courts in Cook County, Illinois and San Francisco County, California (herein after the state/RAND data). Both series are corrected for inflation by converting to Year 2000 dollars. The mean award in the Federal data is about 2.5 times as large as the mean state award. To make the trends clear, the state/RAND awards are graphed against the left axis and the Federal awards against the right axis. Both series show a dramatic increases in mean awards in the 1980s. The roots of the "tort crisis," many observers argue, date back to the 1960s and 1970s when tort law began to move from a negligence standard to a strict liability standard as a means of increasing compensation for the injured (Priest 1991). This explanation may be correct, but, if so, the change in the standard had little effect on the size of tort awards until the mid-1980s. From 1980 to 1990 the mean inflation-adjusted award increased by an average of 8.2 percent a year in the state data and by an average of 17.4 percent a year in the Federal data.

Most cases do not go to trial. Because trials are just the tip of the litigation iceberg, some people have worried that trial data may misrepresent what has happened in the system as a whole. Unfortunately, for most disputes no information on settlements is collected. But we do have good information on settlements for medical malpractice cases in Florida since 1975 and nationally since 1990. Figure 3 shows that medical malpractice settlements increased from about $75,000 in 1980 to more than $250,000 in 1990 and declined mildly in the late 1990s. (Both figures are corrected for inflation by converting to Year 2000 dollars.) At the national level awards also increased in the 1990s, by approximately 40 percent in inflation-adjusted dollars. We emphasize that *Figure 3 is the hidden part of the iceberg*; these are settlements, not trial awards, and therefore are not subject to the argument that higher trial awards are due to a changing selection of cases, rather than to a more generous litigation system.

A related measure, the number of tort filings per capita, also sug-

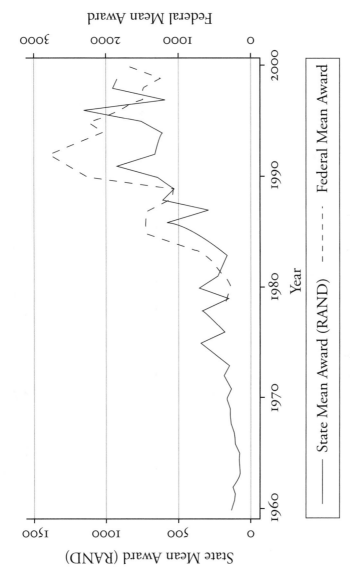

FIGURE 2 State and Federal Trial Awards Are Rising (in $1000). Source: The state data are from Seabury, Pace and Reville, 2004. The Federal data are from the Administrative Office of the U.S. Courts. All awards corrected for inflation and presented in year 2000 dollars.

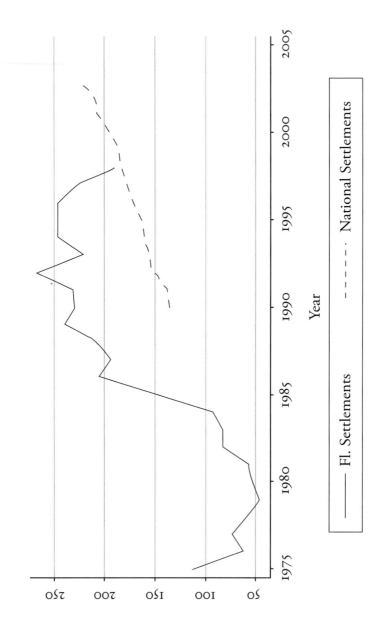

FIGURE 3 Medical Malpractice Settlements Are Rising (in $1000). Source: The Florida series is from The Florida Department of Financial Services Closed Claims File. The national series is single payment settlements from the National Practitioner Data Bank. Both series are corrected for inflation using year 2000 dollars.

gests an increase in the size of the civil justice system. Figure 4 shows the number of filings per 1,000 people in sixteen states between 1975 and 2000 and the number of filings in a larger sample of thirty states from 1993 to 2002.

For the sixteen states for which we have good data, filings increased dramatically in the mid-1980s before leveling off slowly in the 1990s. Much of this decline appears to be caused by California and Florida, which each enacted extensive tort reforms in the 1970s, but due to litigation (of course!), the reforms were not implemented until much later. The shorter series covering more states shows no decline in the 1990s, thus suggesting that while filings declined in some states, they increased in others.

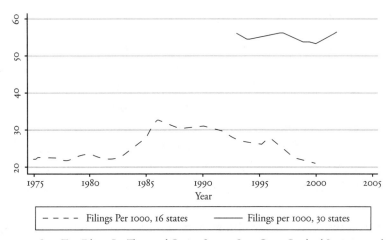

FIGURE 4 State Tort Filings Per Thousand Capita. Source: State Court Caseload Statistics produced by the National Center for the State Courts. The longer series, 1975–2000, covers 16 states: AK, CA, CO, FL, HI, ID, KS, ME, MD, MI, NC, OH, TN, TX, UT, and WA. The shorter series, 1993–2002, adds AR, AZ, CT, IN, MA, MN, MO, NV, NJ, NY, ND, OR, PR, and WI.

SUMMARY OF THE TORT "EXPLOSION"

Whether we look at expenditures, awards, settlements, or filings, the basic story is consistent: The tort system in the United States expanded significantly during the 1970s and 1980s. Whether one calls this an "explosion" or a "litigation hell," as *Newsweek* did, is a matter of personal taste, but either appellation is consistent with the data showing a large and costly increase in the tort system during these two decades. In recent years, this growth has slowed. The retrenchment, however, is a likely consequence of the reform movement and not a reason to regard reform as unnecessary.

What caused the expansion in the tort system? Because this topic has occupied countless law review articles and books, we provide only a cursory sketch here (see Priest 1989 and 1991).

WHY THE EXPANSION?

Tort law traditionally covered injuries between strangers, such as those involved in an automobile accident. Injuries resulting from the interaction between individuals with a prior relationship, such as physicians and patients or workers and employers, were covered by contract law. Contract law let individuals define, prior to any accident, the terms the court would use to resolve disputes. In all other cases, historically, individuals were responsible for paying for their own injuries or received compensation from government-sponsored programs.

This division of responsibility between the tort system, contracts, and private insurance has much to recommend it. It limits the involvement of the courts to non-contractual areas; that is, to instances where one person has potentially harmed another and the parties could not have formed a contract in advance of the injury. In essence, the court's job was to decide whether the defendant was at fault (i.e., liable) and decide on the compensation scheme that the parties to the accident would have agreed to if anonymity had not prevented them from forming such a contract.

Prior to the 1960s, legal cases assigned liability for an injury by applying the *negligence standard*: Did the defendant exercise the care of a reasonable person under the circumstances? As recently as the early 1960s, ladder manufacturers would not have been liable for falls from ladders, doctors would not have been liable for birth defects, and diving board manufacturers would not have been liable for injuries resulting from diving (Priest 1991, p. 38).

The purview of tort law, in terms of which injuries are now potentially compensated, has changed since the 1960s. Some of the changes concern the standard of care that triggers compensation. Although some tort cases, such as those alleging medical malpractice, still use the negligence standard (albeit a much broader standard than was used before the 1960s), others, such as product-liability cases, are now generally decided using *strict liability*. In cases decided using a strict-liability standard, defendants are held responsible for any product-related injuries caused by a product defect, regardless of negligence. The move toward strict liability in product-liability cases and the expansion of what is considered a product defect has brought more injuries into the tort system (Viscusi 1991, p. 73).

Tort law traditionally represented a very limited form of ex-post insurance against the negligent actions of others. Compensation was triggered only by a clearly defined set of deviant actions. Since the 1960s, tort's function has shifted implicitly from punishing negligent actors (with the aim of deterring future injuries) to mandating that producers, in effect, bundle their product with a peculiar form of insurance. Potential litigants are also limited in their ability to avoid tort liability. Court decisions have held that a producer must compensate consumers for all losses resulting from a product without regard to what the parties had specified in advance. By the 1970s, all the legal elements were in place to expand the number of injuries that would end up in the tort system.

Although it is difficult to measure, the changes in legal standards seem to have been accompanied by a greater willingness of the courts to consider claims that previously would have been thought laughable. Jason Love is a good humorist and when he drew this cartoon shortly after the infamous hot-coffee case[6] in August of 1994, his audience probably laughed. Imagine, someone suing McDonald's for obesity! Today such a possibility is no joke. Suits against fast food companies are now common (e.g., *Pelman v. McDonald's*; see also Bradford 2003, and the website of obseity lawyer, John Banzhaf, http://banzhaf.net/obesitylinks).

Inspired by the hot coffee ruling, Bob decides to sue McDonalds for his obesity.

FIGURE 5 Jason Love Cartoon, 1994.

THE COST AND BENEFITS OF THE TORT SYSTEM

The tort system has grown significantly in size and cost over the past decades. But we should not assume that the expansion is necessarily to be decried. We also spend more on health care and more on video games than we did in years past, but neither development is a problem if we receive value for money. Similarly, if the civil justice system works well, then greater use of the system may be a net benefit.

The tort system has two primary functions: It compensates the injured, and it deters injurers. How well does the system perform these two functions? We begin by examining the issue of compensation. An interesting indication—and perhaps an indictment of the tort system—comes from the September 11 Victim Compensation Fund. Congress created the fund to avoid tort law, and nearly every family of a person killed in the 9/11 attacks chose to participate in the fund, voluntarily giving up their rights under tort law. Of course, the 9/11 fund was a response to a unique event. We do not know whether future disasters, man-made or otherwise, will lead to the creation of similar funds. Similar funds have been created, however, for those few children injured by pediatric vaccines. Some states now have no-fault auto insurance. Workers' compensation, basically no-fault accident insurance for on-the-job accidents, has long been a staple of the American workplace. Why would anyone want to give up their right to sue? The primary motivation behind these reforms is the large administrative costs of the tort system: lawyer fees and other expenses push administrative costs to 54 percent of benefits (Tillinghast-Towers Perrin 2003; Economic Report of the President 2004; Hensler 1991). No-fault systems have lower transaction costs and deliver payments to victims sooner than does the tort system.

THE ADMINISTRATIVE COST OF ALTERNATIVE SYSTEMS

More generally, the tort system can be compared with other compensation systems, such as health insurance and workers' compensation. Compensation systems can be broadly classified by what triggers compensation. Even today, the tort system is primarily fault-based; it does not compensate the injured party unless someone else was negligent or in some other way liable. But if you are injured in an accident, you want compensation whether you were hit by a drunk driver or your vehicle skidded out while you were driving alone on an empty road. As a compensation system, therefore, the fault-based tort system is defective—this is one reason why reformers in the 1960s and 1970s pushed for strict liability. Under a strict-liability standard, the injured party is paid even if the "injurer" was not negligent. But what to do with the driver who skids out on an empty road? It's simple—look for someone, anyone, who can pay. Perhaps the auto-manufacturer could (or should?) have included a better braking system? Or maybe the tires were defective? Or perhaps the local government should have better lit that section of road? Notice that the drive to adequately compensate the injured pushes against the fault aspect of tort in two ways: The idea of negligence is weakened, and the number of actors who may be considered liable is expanded and extended.

By contrast, a cause-based system is one in which the specific cause of the injury entitles an individual to compensation. The largest cause-based program in the United States is workers' compensation, which pays for many workplace injuries regardless of whether or not the employer was negligent. Finally, loss-based systems pay compensation based simply on the claimant being injured or ill. These include private loss-based systems such as private health insurance and public systems such as Medicare.

Table 1 places the tort system in context with other systems for compensating injuries. The tort system is considerably less important to overall compensation than private, first-party health insurance companies or Medicaid and Medicare.

Tort awards and other methods of compensation overlap considerably. Studies from the mid-1970s found that 40 percent of all payments to victims made by product-liability insurers involved injured workers who were already entitled to workers' compensation (Dewees 1996, p. 430). It is quite possible that a similar overlap exists between tort compensation and private health insurance in states that do not explicitly allow juries to consider a plaintiff's other sources of compensation when awarding damages. Nevertheless, tort cases are no more than 7 percent of annual expenditures on injuries and illness. If we include only economic damages such as lost wages and exclude noneconomic damages for pain and suffering, the number falls to 3.3 percent—a share comparable to that of the workers' compensation system. The tort system is not the principal way in which the costs of injuries are paid. Moreover, it is important to point out that no one would rely on the tort system as their "primary insurer" to protect them against injury. The scope of tort insurance is narrow and the payout uncertain and delayed.

Although it is not one of the largest compensation systems, the tort system is one of the most costly in terms of the percentage of each dollar spent on administrative overhead. Blue Cross-Blue Shield health insurance has administrative costs that are 10 percent of the benefits it pays out; Social Security disability has administrative costs that are 8 percent of its benefits; and workers' compensation is considered expensive at an average administrative cost that amounts to 20 percent to 21 percent of the benefits it pays. By contrast, the tort system has administrative costs of 54 percent of benefits. For every dollar paid by defendants, only 46 cents goes to the injured party. Thirty-three cents are given to the legal fees generated by plaintiffs' lawyers and defense attorneys and 21 cents is due to other administrative overhead costs, such as the cost of distributing insurance payments.

Compensation is desirable, but the tort system is an odd horse to bear that burden. The tort system is a continually evolving jumble of fault-based and strict-liability standards that do not fit easily with the goal of low-cost compensation

The high administrative costs of the system, moreover, are probably inevitable, given that compensation comes from a specific individual or organization that will always have an incentive to contest the decision. Imagine, for example, a tort-like system for providing the funds necessary for national defense. If we needed a new airplane fleet, for example, the federal government might sue Boeing to provide it for free. Boeing would claim that Raytheon should be

TABLE 1 Compensation for Injury, Illness, and Fatality in the United States (2001).[A]

Type of Injury or Illness Compensation System		Amount ($ billions)	Percentage of total
Fault-based	Tort Economic Payment[B] (2002)	$41	3.33%
	Tort Non-Economic Payment[C] (2002)	$41.50	3.37%
Cause-based	Workers Compensation[D]	$48.70	3.96%
	No-Fault Auto Insurance	$11	0.89%
	Black Lung Benefits	$0.48	0.04%
	Veterans' Benefits[E]	$26.50	2.15%
Loss-based	Private First-Party Insurance		
	Health Insurance[F]	$426.50	34.66%
	Life Insurance[G]	$45.40	3.69%
	Disability Insurance	$10.20	0.83%
	Social/Public Insurance		
	Medicaid and Medicare[H]	$427.70	34.76%
	Medicaid Prescription Drug[I]	$14.70	1.19%
	Other Federal and State	$44.80	3.64%
	Disability		
	SSD[J], SSI[K]	$92	7.48%
Total		$1,230	100%

Social Security Administration. *Annual Statistical Report on the Social Security Disability Insurance Program, 2002.* 2002.

Tillinghast-Towers Perrin. *U.S. Tort Costs: 2003 Update. Trends and Findings on the Costs of the U.S. Tort System.* 2003.

U.S. Census Bureau. *Statistical Abstract of the United States* (2002). 2003.

[A] Denominated in billions. Used Table B-60 of 2003 ERP (page 345) for conversion to 2001 constant dollars. Adjusted for inflation using Consumer Price Index for all urban consumers; 1982–84=100.

[B] Tillinghast Study: 20% of $205 billion

[C] Tillinghast Study: 22% of 205 billion.

[D] Census Statistical Abstract of 2002. Chart No. 532 Excludes black lung benefits financed from general appropriations revenue. Glen King, U.S. Department of Census unpublished data for 2001.

[E] Census Statistical Abstract of 2002. Chart No. 510 Glen King, U.S. Department of Census unpublished data for 2001.

[F] Health Insurance Association of America. Source Book of Health Insurance Data (2002). Table 1.1

[G] American Council of Life Insurers. Life Insurance Fact Book (2002). Table 5.

[H] Health Insurance Association of America. Source Book of Health Insurance Data (2002). Table 4.6

[I] Health Insurance Association of America. Source Book of Health Insurance Data (2002). Table 4.11

[J] Social Security Administration. *Annual Statistical Report on the Social Security Disability Insurance Program.* Total Annual Benefit Payments $60 billion.

[K] Social Security Administration. *SSI Annual Statistical Report 2001.* Total Annual Benefit Payments $32 billion.

required to pay for the planes, and if Boeing lost the case, it would have to cover its losses by raising prices to other Boeing customers, by reducing wages or by declaring bankruptcy. The example may seem fanciful, yet this is exactly what has happened in many asbestos-liability cases (Stiglitz, Orszag, and Orszag 2002). Providing the planes through the tort system would appear to be much less efficient than simply raising the funds through general taxes and buying the planes.[7] So why not provide compensation to injured parties in exactly the same way? The answer, to the extent that there is one, must be deterrence.

DETERRENCE

If most injuries are not paid for by the tort system, and the tort system is an expensive way of compensating victims, then why have a tort system at all? Why not rely on insurance and other forms of compensation as do other countries? The tort system makes sense only if it provides significant deterrence. Unfortunately, it appears that in areas such as product liability and medical malpractice, the tort system is not delivering large enough deterrence benefits to justify its higher administrative costs, *at least given the size of the current system*. For example, a study of heart patients found that state laws that capped awards in medical malpractice cases caused a reduction in expenditures on treatment but had a minimal effect on the mortality rate of the heart patients (Kessler and McClellan, 1996, 2002). In addition, the possibility of a malpractice suit induces potential defendants to take costly actions that will limit their liability exposure but may not reduce the likelihood or cost of accidents. The performance of unnecessary or low-value medical procedures, such as unwarranted caesarian births or additional tests that are not medically necessary, has been labeled "defensive medicine."

Studies examining injury rates for consumers and workers and death rates from medical procedures and workplace injuries show no more rapid decline in the 1980s than in the 1970s, despite the increase in litigation (Priest 1989). Several studies examine the deterrence aspect of medical-malpractice liability by estimating the consequences of limitations on damage awards. These studies find little or no adverse impacts on treatment outcome (Kessler and McClellan 1991; Durby, 1999, 2001). Similarly, a study of punitive damages found no evidence that allowing such damages has an effect on environmental or safety torts relative to the four states that do not allow punitive damages (Viscusi 1998).

Comparisons of accident rates and tort expenditures across countries also do not support a strong deterrence effect. Figure 6 plots tort expenditures as a percentage of GDP against accidental death rates for 12 advanced countries. If the tort system were deterring many accidents, we would expect to see a downward sloping curve—greater tort expenditures leading to fewer accidents. Instead, what we see is a flat line—no relationship at all between expenditures and accident rates. The United States is notable only for having tort expenditures that are nearly twice as high as the average country but accident rates that are no lower than average.

Of course, many other factors can influence accident rates, so the figure doesn't prove that the tort system does not deter. But it does suggest that if we want to reduce accidents, we ought to look elsewhere than the tort system—even large changes in expenditures don't appear to produce large changes in accident rates.

Product liability and medical liability may actually *reduce* safety if the increases in price that result from greater liability risk *reduce* the purchases of safety-improving products (Rubin and Shepherd 2005). In the early 1980s, for example, pediatric vaccine developers started to be sued extensively. Figure 7 shows how a rush of lawsuits increased the price of the DPT (Diphtheria, Pertussis, Tetanus) vaccine from under $10 in 1980 to more than $150 in 1987. For various reasons, the lawsuits focused on the Pertussis portion of the DPT

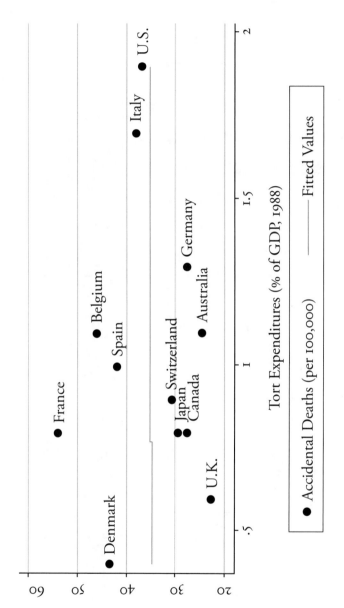

Tort Expenditures (% of GDP, 1988)

● Accidental Deaths (per 100,000) ——— Fitted Values

FIGURE 6 Tort Expenditures versus Accidental Deaths. Source: Tort Expenditures from Tillinghast-Towers Perrin. 2003. U.S. Tort Costs: 2003 Update. Accident Rates for Denmark, U.K., France, Switzerland, Spain, Belgium, Germany, Italy from Eurostat, 1988. Accident rates for Canada from Statistics Canada, 1998. Accident Rates for Japan, Australia from International Accident Facts, 2002. Accident Rates for United States from Statistical Abstract of the United States, 1999.

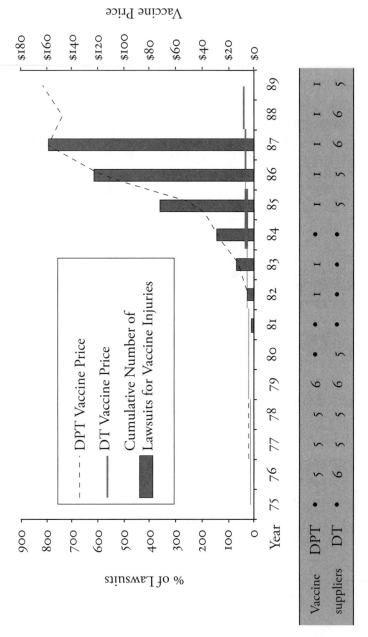

FIGURE 7 Vaccine Litigation Caused the Price of DPT to Skyrocket. Source: Manning (1994).

vaccine, so the DT vaccine was less subject to suits. Thus, the difference between the prices of the two vaccines illustrates the effect of lawsuits after controlling for other common cost factors. Almost all of the price increase of the DPT vaccine was caused by lawsuits.

Given the tremendous benefits of childhood vaccines, any policy that raised the price and reduced the quantity of vaccines available would have to show offsetting benefits on a similar scale. Thus far, such benefits have not been demonstrated. Indeed, several pharmaceutical companies left the industry, and now the United States is subject to recurring shortages of pediatric vaccines that save lives.

The tort system is not the only system for deterrence. The Federal Drug Administration (FDA), for example, operates an extensive system of pre-market regulatory review to improve the safety of pharmaceuticals and medical devices. Adding the tort system on top of the FDA may, in fact, over-deter the production of new pharmaceuticals. Other regulatory systems monitor the safety of appliances, automobiles, children's toys, and many other goods and services. As with pharmaceutical regulation, the tort system could be a good alternative to regulatory systems, but it is difficult to see why it should be an addition to regulatory systems.

Moreover, even without regulation or tort, the market provides producers of goods and services with powerful financial incentives to make their products safer, at least when the safety of their customers is at stake. Companies whose products cause injuries suffer considerable market penalties from the loss of business (Jarrell and Peltzman 1985).

Another possible reason for the lack of deterrence in medical-malpractice and product-liability cases is that the current tort system makes it hard to predict which actions will be deemed negligent. Most people on a jury and most judges understand intuitively what constitutes reckless driving, but understanding how a 20-year-old aircraft should have been built stretches the ability of most laymen.[8] Furthermore, in an auto accident it is relatively easy to see that had

X not done Y, the injury would not have occurred, but in a medical malpractice, it is often the case that even if X had done A, B, C, or D, instead of Y, the injury would still have occurred. Juries are not good at accurately incorporating information about background risk into their liability calculations, a problem Viscusi and Zeckhauser (2004) label the "denominator blindness effect." Deterrence doesn't work well if juries cannot identify who should be deterred and defendants cannot predict who will be punished.

OUTLINE OF THE BOOK

In this book, we examine three of the key players in the tort system: juries, judges, and lawyers. Chapter 2 takes up the question we asked above: Does "the Bronx effect" redistribute wealth? More generally, do jury awards vary by jury characteristics such as wealth and race? We find evidence that Tom Wolfe's insight was correct—awards are much higher in counties that have high rates of black and Hispanic poverty.

The United States is one of the few remaining countries in the world to rely extensively on juries in civil cases. Should the United States move instead to a judge-dominated system? How do the average jury and the average judge compare? Comparing judge and jury behavior is more difficult than it sounds because judges and juries see different types of cases. Thus, a proper comparison must control for case composition and other factors. In Chapter 3, we find that after controlling for factors such as case composition, judges and juries differ much less than is commonly believed. Perhaps it is not surprising that the problems in the current system can't be laid solely at the feet of juries. It was judges and lawyers, not juries, who drove the changes in the law that expanded the tort system.

Even if we thought that judges are preferable to juries, not all judges are the same. Federal judges are appointed for life, but many judges in state courts, where most tort law action occurs, are elected, and quite a few run in elections that can be just as partisan, expensive, and highly contested as Congressional elections. Where do elected judges get their campaign funds? Where do they get their votes? What effect does this judicial electoral system have on tort awards? Chapter 4 looks at how tort awards vary by judicial electoral system. We find strong evidence that partisan-elected judges redistribute awards from out-of-state companies to in-state plaintiffs and their lawyers. Perhaps judges are not immune to the same forces that can bias juries.

Chapters 2 and 4 explain why "forum shopping" among lawyers (i.e., looking for the right time and place to sue) is so common and so profitable. Jury awards are higher in regions with high minority poverty rates and higher in states with partisan-elected judges. No wonder that a state like Alabama, where it's possible to find counties with both high minority poverty rates and partisan-elected judges, has been called a "tort hell."

Chapter 5 takes up the third major player in the tort system: lawyers. Tort reformers often blame the explosion in tort awards on lawyers and frivolous lawsuits brought on by contingency fees. It is true that the United States is one of the few countries to allow lawyers to be paid with contingent fees; although, other countries like Britain and Canada appear to be moving more in favor of the U.S. system. But contingent fees have been used in the United States for more than 100 years. It seems surprising, therefore, that they should cause trouble only in the last thirty years. Restrictions on contingency fees are really restrictions on plaintiffs' and lawyers' freedom to contract, and restrictions on the freedom to contract often have unexpected and unintended consequences. Chapter 5 looks at one such unintended consequence: restrictions on contingency fees encourage lawyers to take on cases without regard to the quality of the cases. In one sense, therefore, restrictions on contingency fees have increased the number of frivolous lawsuits!

Chapter 6 takes up the issue of reform. What can or should be done about the problems that we document? Are award caps a good idea? Should tort law be federalized? Should we abandon tort law altogether? Unfortunately, it's easier to study how the current system operates than to design new systems, but empirical research does offer some guidance as to what has worked in the past and what might work in the future.

2

Race, Poverty, and American Tort Awards

Television journalist Morley Safer of CBS's *60 Minutes* introduced "Jackpot Justice," a story about the tort system, this way:

> It's been nicknamed Jackpot Justice. It's about where lawyers like to go when they sue big corporations for personal injury. It's not to the big cities where the corporations are headquartered but to places like, for example, rural, impoverished, Jefferson County, Mississippi. Why Mississippi? Well plaintiffs' lawyers have found that juries in rural impoverished places can be mighty sympathetic when one of their own goes up against a big, rich multinational corporation.[1]

Jefferson County, Mississippi, is a small, poor, rural county with a population of just over 9,000; 86.5 percent of the population is black and more than one-third of the county population lives below the poverty line.[2] Despite its small size, Jefferson County is home to lots of lawsuits. Between 1995 and 2000, more than 21,000 lawsuits were filed in Jefferson County—an average of two suits per person (Pear 2001)! A number of these suits and settlements have resulted in multi-million dollar awards leading some to call Jefferson County a "lawsuit Mecca."[3]

Anecdotes like those appearing on *60 Minutes* are not uncommon. As we noted in the introduction, Tom Wolfe has written about the Bronx jury as a means of "redistributing the wealth." Similarly, McClellan (1996, p. 764) makes the provocative argument that "the only institutions in America where people of color have the power to make immediate wealth redistribution decisions are urban governments and juries." Although anecdotes may hint at an interesting phenomena, they do not substitute for evidence, and prior to our study no systematic evidence on race, poverty, and tort awards had ever been established.[4]

THE DATA

This chapter reports results from three data sets. The primary data set was extracted from Jury Verdict Research's (hereafter JVR) *Personal Injury Verdicts and Settlements* on CD-ROM. The JVR data set contains information on 122,444 trials, settlements, and arbitrations. The earliest cases were tried in 1988, and the most recent date from 1996. All award amounts are corrected for inflation by conversion into 1996 dollars. We are interested in the effect of jury demographics on tort awards, so we focus our attention on the 42,315 trials, coming from 1,803 counties, which resulted in a plaintiff win.[5] The JVR data set is useful because of its large size and because it contains information on the case type (product liability, medical malpractice, sexual harassment, premises liability, etc.) and on the plaintiff's injuries, which lets us control for a wide range of factors other than those of direct interest. The bulk of the cases (75%) are in auto accident cases (51%), premises liability (14%), medical malpractice (7%), or product liability (4%) cases. We exclude cases in the JVR data that were tried before a judge. For more on the data used in this study see Helland, Klick, and Tabarrok 2005.[6]

To verify results from the JVR data set we examine two other data sets. The first is from the Civil Justice Survey of State Courts (1992). The State Courts data set is slightly broader than the JVR data set as it covers tort, contract, and real property cases. All the cases were disposed of between July 1, 1991, and June 30, 1992, in forty-five counties chosen to represent the seventy-five most populous counties in the nation (these counties account for about half of all civil filings). The data set is distributed by the Inter-University Consortium for Political and Social Research (ICPSR 6,587). The State Courts data set has information on 3,199 trials with positive awards. It contains some case-type data, but does not contain the extensive injury information found in the JVR data. The main defect of the data set is its relatively small size (the number of State Courts cases examined is only 7.6 percent of the number of cases JVC examined) and the small number of counties represented (forty-five). The advantage of the State Courts data is that it is designed to be a random sample of trial awards.

The second supplementary data set covers Federal court cases. The data are gathered by the Administrative Office of the United States Courts, assembled by the Federal Judicial Center, and disseminated by the Inter-University Consortium for Political and Social Research (ICPSR, 8,429).[7] The data set is more restrictive than either the JVR or State Courts data. First, and most importantly, federal courts draw juries from districts and divisions within districts rather than by county. We call the geographic area from which a federal trial draws a jury a "trial unit." Trial units can range from single counties to subsets of counties to entire states. Trial units, however, never divide a county. Thus, using demographic data on counties, we can aggregate upward to create a population-weighted demographic data set for each Federal trial unit. For example, Alabama is divided into the Northern, Middle, and Southern Districts, and each of these districts is further divided into divisions; each division comprises a number of counties which are listed in the U.S. Code (Title 28). In other cases, however, the U.S. Code does not subdivide districts into divisions, but it does require that courts be held in listed cities. In these states, local court rules rather than the federal code determine which counties comprise the trial unit for each of the listed federal courts.[8]

Because federal trial units are larger than counties, the variation in poverty rates is less than at the county level. If demographic effects exist, they will be more difficult to detect in the Federal data than in the State data. Nevertheless, as our findings are likely to be controversial, we wish to examine as many different sources of data as possible.[9]

The bulk of federal court cases concern federal matters rather than disputes between individuals or individuals and companies. We restrict the Federal data set to cases broadly similar in type to those in the JVR and State Courts data sets—essentially personal-injury torts, most of which arise through diversity jurisdictions (i.e., suits between parties who live in different states). As with the JVR data, we exclude cases that are tried before a judge. County poverty rates are available only in census years, so we focus on court cases from 1988 to 1992, thus bracketing the census year 1990 by two years on each side. This bracketing gives us a data set of just under 5,000 cases. It is worth noting that regardless of our selection, Federal cases are likely to be quite different than state court cases. In addition, as mentioned above, our unit of analysis in the Federal data, the trial unit, is different than the county. Thus, we should not necessarily expect the coefficients to be the same size in all three data sets, but we would expect the same signs.

Because the JVR data set is larger than the Federal or State Courts data sets, we are able to break down the data by case type. The JVR data also has more control variables. Thus, we will use the JVR data as our primary data set, and where possible the Federal Court data and the State Courts data will be used to check for robustness. As with the JVR data, all award amounts in the Federal Court and the State Courts data are converted into 1996 dollars.

We supplement the data on trials with data on county demographics drawn from the 1990 census. We hypothesize that awards vary with county demographics because awards vary with jury composition and jury composition varies with county demographics. The most important limitation of the data sets, however, is that we must infer the average composition of the jury from county demographics. The inference is plausible so long as there is a positive relationship between county and jury demographics—in other words, provided that an increase in the proportion of the county's population that is black (poor, Hispanic, etc.) also tends to increase the proportion of jury members who are black (poor, Hispanic, etc.) The assumption might have been questionable in the 1960s when jury selection procedures in some parts of the country were designed to exclude blacks and other minorities from jury duty, but modern selection procedures are designed to ensure that such a positive relationship exists.[10, 11]

Although we think it plausible that jury demographics are the causal force behind the correlations we find between average awards by county and county demographics, it should be clear that this is a hypothesis. In Chapter 3, we discuss an interesting piece of evidence in support of this hypothesis—awards given by juries increase in county poverty rates but not awards given by judges. We do not attempt, however, to solve the "ecological inference" problem. Further research will be necessary to precisely identify the causal forces behind the correlations that we document.

RESULTS

EXPLORING THE DATA: POVERTY RATES AND TORT AWARDS

In Table 1, we split the trial awards into seven groups according to the 1990 poverty rate of the county in which the trial occurred.[12] All trial awards that occurred in a county with a poverty rate of between 0 percent and 5 percent are in Group 1, trial awards that occurred in a county with a poverty rate of between 5 percent and 10 percent are in Group 2 and so forth. (Each group has a poverty range of 5 percent except for the final group, which includes counties with poverty rates of 35 percent or more.) The data show a marked increase in award by poverty rate. As the average county poverty rate increases from 4.1 percent to 21.9 percent, for example, the average award triples from just over $400,000 to just over $1.3 million.

For verification, Tables 2 and 3 report the same experiment using the State Courts and Federal data, respectively. Because these data sets cover fewer counties than does the JVR data set, the poverty range is lower. Although the average awards tend to be lower in the State Courts data than in the JVR data set, it is clear that the rate of increase with respect to poverty is similar. Awards in federal court, however, do not appear to increase strongly with poverty. Figure 1 plots the data from Tables 1, 2, and 3.

Regression results, shown in Table 4, strengthen the impression given by Figure 1. The regression estimates are very similar across the JVR and State Courts data sets; a 1 percentage point increase in poverty rates increases awards by approximately $35,300 in the JVR data set and by $33,700 in the State Courts data set.[13] The regression results also suggest a positive, albeit smaller, effect of poverty in the Federal data. A 1 percentage point increase in poverty is estimated to increase awards by $18,854 in the Federal data set. All the results are highly statistically significant (greater than 1% level).[14, 15]

Examining the JVR data in another way we calculate the probability that an award will be $1 million or larger is 10 percent, 20 percent, and 35 percent in low, medium, and high-poverty counties, respectively. (Recall that these awards are conditional upon winning.)[16]

Table 5 breaks the JVR data down into product liability, medical malpractice and auto cases (the other two data sets are too small to examine subsets). The poverty rate increases awards much more in product-liability cases and medical-malpractice cases than in auto cases. That is, not only are awards higher in product-liability and

TABLE 1 Mean Tort Awards by Poverty Rate, JVR Data.

Poverty Range	Mean Poverty Rate in Range	Mean Award	No. Observations
0–5%	4.1%	$398,874	2,714
5–10%	7.5%	$470,875	10,373
10–15%	12.5%	$647,882	16,018
15–20%	17.4%	$670,597	8,915
20–25%	21.9%	$1,185,010	3,150
25–30%	27.8%	$1,185,630	1,031
35%+	40%	$2,661,910	114
0–100%	12.8%	$651,241	42,315[A]

[A]Slight differences in the number of observations between the sample statistics and regressions are due to missing observations on independent variables.

TABLE 2 Mean Tort Awards by Poverty Rate, State Court Data, 1996 Dollars.

Poverty Range	Mean Poverty Rate in Range	Mean Award	No. Observations
0–5%	3.6%	$126,987	199
5–10%	7.6%	$260,529	858
10–15%	13.1%	$547,978	934
15–20%	17%	$664,435	628
20–25%	20.4%	$758,347	487
0–100%	12.9%	$498,131	3,106

TABLE 3 Mean Tort Awards by Poverty Rate, Federal Court Data, 1996 Dollars.

Poverty Range	Mean Poverty Rate in Range	Mean Award	No. Observations
0–10%	7.9%	$1,024,247	891
10–15%	11.6%	$1,081,002	2,112
15–20%	17.1%	$1,586,245	965
20–25%	22%	$1,003,034	659
25–100%	29%	$1,331,389	157
0–100%	14%	$1,169,823	4,784

TABLE 4 Regression Results, Total Awards on Poverty, JVR, and State Court Data.

	JVR Data	State Court Data	Federal Court Data
Constant	187,066*	65,177	920,838*
	(38,967)	(100,292)	(108,956)
Poverty Rate	36,864*	33,476*	18,854*
	(3,340)	(10,018)	(7,115)
Observations	41,150	3,106	4,784

* Significant at greater than 1% level.

** Significant at greater than 5% level.

Standard errors are robust (heterosecadastic-consistent). Federal regression using interval/censored procedure to handle bottom and top-coding.

medical-malpractice cases, but the rate of increase of awards with respect to county poverty is larger. Figure 2 summarizes these findings in a diagram.

Helland and Tabarrok (1999) show that the average award in product-liability and medical-malpractice cases is higher than in auto cases, even when injuries are held constant. An alternative way of stating the results of Table 5 and Figure 2 is that the markup for product-liability and medical-malpractice cases is much smaller in low-poverty counties than in high-poverty counties.

FURTHER RESULTS: RACE AND POVERTY

The strong and positive relationship between poverty rates and tort awards raises a number of questions. Due to the high rate of poverty among blacks, black population rates and all-population poverty rates are highly correlated (0.46 in the Federal data, 0.53 in the JVR data, and 0.58 in the State Courts data). To a lesser but still significant extent, Hispanic population rates and all-population poverty rates are also correlated (0.2 Federal, 0.33 JVR, and 0.27 State Courts). It's possible, therefore, that poverty is too narrow a variable and is picking up results more properly ascribed to black and/or Hispanic popu-

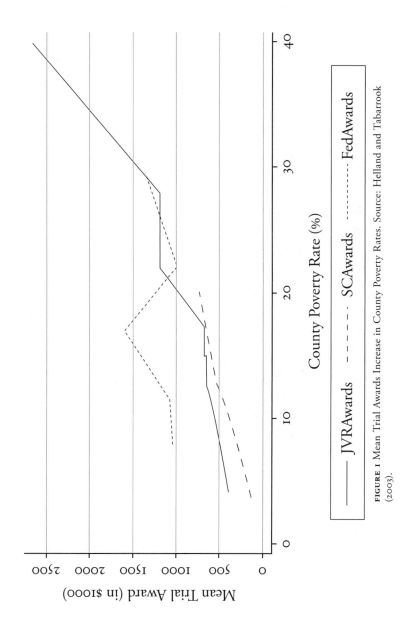

FIGURE 1 Mean Trial Awards Increase in County Poverty Rates. Source: Helland and Tabarrook (2003).

TABLE 5 Mean Awards by County Poverty Rate in Product Liability, Medical Malpractice and Auto Cases, JVR Data.

Poverty Range	Product Liability Mean	Obs	Med. Malpractice Mean	Obs	Auto Cases Mean	Obs
0–5%	$1,183,410	57	$1,077,330	262	$243,670	1,590
5–10%	$2,279,620	313	$1,480,071	601	$228,613	5,797
10–15%	$1,929,380	675	$1,806,510	1,083	$280,056	8,124
15–20%	$2,485,990	512	$1,811,420	559	$240,540	4,103
20–25%	$4,279,320	138	$3,105,800	272	$544,865	1,414
25%+	$6,743,680	45	$4,001,020	72	$759,719	525
0–100%	$2,441,440	1,769	$1,851,190	2,849	$285,069	21,553

lations of all income levels. Or, it may be that poverty is too broad a variable and that it is picking up results more properly ascribed to low-income black or Hispanic populations.

Regression results in Table 6 attempt to distinguish and evaluate these possibilities. We are interested in the demographics of the *jury pool* thus we would like to measure, for example, the number of jury-age blacks relative to the total jury-age population. The readily available Census data breaks the age population into divisions such as ages 15–19 and ages 20–24. Using these divisions we created age 20-plus (i.e. age 20 and older) population figures for the black, Hispanic and "white" populations.[17] Note that we define "white" as non-black and non-Hispanic.

The Census has data on the number of blacks and Hispanics in poverty but does not further subdivide these populations by age. We construct a jury-age black poverty rate by multiplying the total number of blacks in the county who are below the poverty line by the ratio of the 20-plus black population to the total black population and then dividing by the total 20-plus population of the county. We do the same thing for Hispanics.

It is important to recognize that the "black poverty rate" in our regressions is *not* the percentage of blacks who are in poverty, but rather the number of in-poverty blacks as a percentage of the coun-

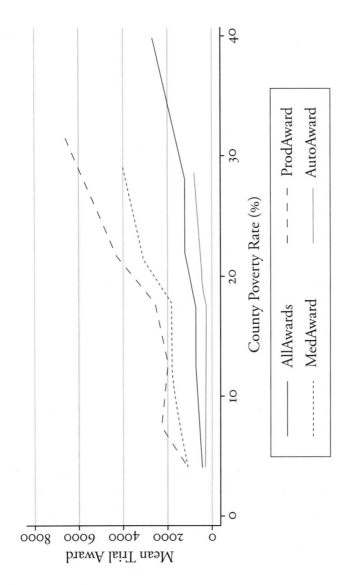

FIGURE 2 Mean Trial Awards Increase in County Poverty Rate in Product Liability, Medical Malpractice and Auto Cases (in $1000). Source: Helland and Tabarrook (2003).

TABLE 6 Regression of Awards on Race and Poverty Variables.

	(1) Poverty only	(2)	(3)	(4) Non-Minority Whites	(5)	(6) State Courts Data	(7) Federal Courts Data
Constant	184,967* (39,055)	109,368 (40,236)	362,752* (42,718)	449,232* (35,018)	330,279 (34,751)	353,102* (124,356)	941,532* (111,541)
Poverty	36,864* (3,353)	12,257* (3,014)	−8,805* (3,245)	−4,768 (2,583)			
Black		11,090* (1,541)	4,150 (4,925)				
Hispanic		17,901* (1,337)	−3,541 (4,046)				
White Poverty Rate					−4,328** (1,836)	−36,198** (15,497)	14,199** (7,108)
Black Poverty Rate			30,666* (17,848)		34,251* (5,370)	32,856* (9,319)	23,033** (9,970)
Hispanic Poverty Rate			172,712* (31,460)		137,725* (11,441)	71,390** (29,235)	18,311 (26,595)
Obs.	41,150	41,150	41,150	12,593	41,150	3,106	4,784

*Significant at greater than 1% level.

**Significant at greater than 5% level.

***Significant at greater than 10% level.

Standard errors are robust (heterosecadastic-consistent)

All awards are in real 1996 dollars.

ty population (both adjusted by age for jury eligibility). Given our working hypothesis that jury composition affects awards, there is a big difference between a county with a 5 percent black population— 50 percent of whom are below the poverty line (a 50 percent black poverty rate in the usual terminology) and a county where 50 percent of the population is black and below the poverty line (a black poverty rate of 50 percent according to our usage).[18]

To ease comparison, Column 1 of Table 6 repeats the regression of total awards on poverty. In Column 2, the share of the voting-age black and Hispanic populations are included alongside poverty. All three variables are statistically and economically significant. Note that the size of the coefficient on poverty drops to about a third of that in the poverty alone regressions, suggesting that poverty alone is picking up results more properly ascribed to some combination of the poverty, black and Hispanic variables. According to the regression, a 1 percentage point increase in the black population raises awards by \$11 thousand while a 1 percentage point increase in the Hispanic population raises awards by nearly \$18 thousand.

Column 3 of Table 6 further distinguishes hypotheses by introducing the black poverty rate and the Hispanic poverty rate as variables. With the inclusion of these variables, the coefficient on poverty becomes negative and significantly so. The results on the race variables are mixed; the coefficient on black is positive while that on Hispanic is negative but neither is close to statistically significant. The black and Hispanic poverty levels, however, are large, positive, and statistically significant. The suggestion, therefore, is that it is poor black and Hispanic populations that increase awards rather than black and Hispanic populations per se. But these results need to be interpreted with caution. As noted above, the poverty rate and the black and Hispanic population rate are highly correlated. The black poverty rate (defined as above) and the black population rate are even more highly correlated (0.93). Similarly for the Hispanic poverty rate and the Hispanic population rate (0.92).

We perform two robustness tests. In Column 4, we remove all counties with black and Hispanic population rates of greater than 10 percent. The remaining 12,458 observations span counties with poverty levels ranging from 2 percent to 62 percent so the sample contains significant variation in county poverty rates. Nevertheless, the coefficient on poverty remains negative. Since counties with large black and Hispanic populations have been removed from Regression 4 (and are controlled for in Regression 3), the negative coefficient on poverty suggests that white poverty (defined as the rate of poverty in the non-black and non-Hispanic populations) is, if anything, *negatively* related to tort awards. We follow up on this observation further below.

Distinguishing the influence of black and Hispanic populations from the influence of black and Hispanic populations in poverty is difficult. In order to make this distinction, we would need a sample of counties with low poverty rates and large percentages of blacks or Hispanics. Unfortunately, there are almost no such counties in the United States (Prince Georges County in Maryland is the only county in the United States with a majority black population and a poverty rate below 10 percent.) The results in Column 3 weakly suggest that black and Hispanic poverty rates are the key variables. In Column 5, we present results from a regression of tort awards on black and Hispanic poverty rates excluding the variables for black and Hispanic populations. In addition, following the findings above, we include the white poverty rate. The results indicate that increases in black and Hispanic poverty rates increase awards but increases in white poverty reduce awards. Bearing in mind that further research will be necessary to convincingly separate the influence of poor black and Hispanic populations from black and Hispanic populations in general, we focus in what follows upon this specification.[19]

A priori, one would expect that awards would *fall* with an increase in county poverty because wages are lower in counties with high poverty levels and compensatory awards should fall with a decline in wages. We find instead that awards rise strongly with black and Hispanic poverty and fall only with white poverty. The wage-effect should be the same in counties with high proportions of poor whites, blacks, or Hispanics. If the coefficient on white poverty is capturing the wage effect, then the increase in awards with black and Hispanic poverty rates is all the more remarkable. In other words, to the extent that white poverty controls for factors such as the wage effect, which may also be operative in other poor counties, the true coefficients on black and Hispanic poverty are larger by the coefficient on white poverty. The difference between the coefficient on white poverty and the ones on black and Hispanic poverty, respectively, may therefore be considered a difference in the difference estimator that controls for any factors correlated with poverty per se.

Columns 6 and 7 of Table 6 present regressions of total awards on white, black and Hispanic poverty in the State Courts and Federal Court data sets. Recall that the State Courts and Federal data set are smaller and in the case of the Federal data, more aggregated, than the JVR data. Taking into account the differences among the data sets, the results appear quite consistent. Awards in all three data sets increase with black and Hispanic poverty rates; although, the Hispanic poverty variable is not significant in the Federal data and the sizes of the effects are smaller. The main difference is that in the Federal data, awards also increase with white poverty rates.

We turn now to a more detailed analysis that attempts to rule out other possible explanations of these findings through the addition of control variables.

INJURIES, CASE TYPES, CITIES, AND FIXED EFFECTS

Controlling for other variables will increase our confidence in any discovered relationship between race, poverty and tort awards. We are able to control for injuries, case types, high-density counties and state-fixed effects. We discuss each of these controls in turn. The JVR data set has descriptive information on the victim's physical injury such as broken arm, lost leg, cancer, blindness, skin rash etc. We code this information into three exclusive and exhaustive dummy variables: Death, Major Injury, and Minor Injury; where Major injuries are defined as those which are permanent (lost leg) and minor are temporary (broken leg, skin rash). In addition we also include variables if the plaintiff claims Emotional Distress, Rape, Sexual Assault, Sexual Harassment, or Wrongful Termination.

Case type variables are Premises Liability, Medical Malpractice, Product Liability, Auto, Employment, and Bad Faith Contracting. The vast majority of cases have both an injury and a case type thus the coefficient on Medical Malpractice or Product Liability gives us the increase in awards in these types of cases holding the injuries variable constant. Some Bad Faith cases can involve a plaintiff suing a health insurance company to force the company to pay for a specific treatment. In these cases, the injury may be only potential and thus is not coded.

For a variety of reasons, we might expect awards to be higher in urban counties or counties that include cities. It may be, for example, that high-profile cases with potentially high awards are litigated more often in urban areas than in rural areas. It could also be that the better or more specialized lawyers are located in high-density population areas. To control for these effects, we include the population density as a regressor. Note that the case-type variables already go some distance to controlling for larger cases, but the population variables will control for any unobserved differences in case types or lawyer quality that are correlated with population density.[20]

State fixed effects are dummy variables specific to each state. To see the importance of including state fixed effects, imagine that there are only two states. The first state has a lot of high-poverty counties and the second state only a few high-poverty counties. Assume that the high-poverty state has high tort awards, but for reasons peculiar to that state and not related to poverty. A regression of awards on poverty will indicate that high poverty rates are associated with high awards. This will occur despite the fact that a high-poverty county in the low-poverty state will not experience unusually high awards. Including state fixed effects separates state effects from poverty effects, thus forcing the coefficient on poverty to indicate the within-state effect of poverty.

Table 7 contains the coefficients on white, black, and Hispanic poverty once injuries, case types, population density and state fixed effects have been controlled for. Despite the inclusion of sixty-four additional variables, the results are consistent with those found earlier. (Results on variables other than those of direct interest may be

TABLE 7 Regression of Total Award on State Fixed Effects, Injury Variables, Case Types, Population Density, and White, Black, and Hispanic Poverty.

	(1) JVR Data[A]	(2) JVR— Logged Awards	(3) State Court Data[B]	(4) State Court Logged Awards	(5) Federal Court Data[C]	(6) Federal Logged Awards
White Poverty Rate	−8,644* (2,876)	−.0038 (.00288)	−18.199 (30,634)	.03854 (.03966)	19,665** (8.209)	.0416* (.0156)
Black Poverty Rate	19,838* (6,762)	.0317* (.0033)	74,991* (21,447)	.1001* (.02169)	18,875* (10,152)	.0743* (.01767)
Hispanic Poverty Rate	78,558* (15,708)	.0717* (.00559)	−106,159 (68,608)	−.0536*** .03197	12,344 (27,405)	.1206* (.0491)
Obs.	41,150	41,150	3,106	3,106	4,784	4,784

*Significant at greater than 1% level.

**Significant at greater than 5% level.

***Significant at greater than 10% level.

[A] Full results for this model may be found in Table A1, results on other models are similar.

[B] Includes a less extensive set of injury variables than the JVR data; also includes case types, density, and state fixed effects. Full results for this model may be found in Helland and Tabarrok 2003.

[C] Does not include injury variables but does include case types, district densities, and year dummy variables.

Standard errors are robust (heterosecadastic-consistent)

All awards are in real 1996 dollars.

found in Helland and Tabarrok 2003). An increase in white poverty rates continues to decrease awards. For example, as we see in Row 1, Column 1, a percentage point increase in white poverty rates decreases awards by $8,644. Similarly, a percentage point increase in black poverty rates raises awards by almost $20,000 and a 1% increase in Hispanic poverty raises average tort awards by over $78,000.

In Column 2 of Table 7, we show the results from a similar regression using logged awards. Since awards can never be lower than zero, but in principle may be infinitely high, logging them reduces the influence of outliers and also allows the relationship between awards and poverty rates to change with the poverty rate. The coefficients on the poverty rates can now be interpreted as the percentage change in awards given a 1 percentage point change in poverty rates.[21] The coefficient on white poverty rates is negative but small and statistically insignificant. A percentage point increase in the black poverty rate raises awards by 3.2 percent and a similar increase in Hispanic poverty rates raises awards by 7.2 percent. Evaluated at the mean winning award ($654,627), an increase of 3.2 percent is $20,948 and 7.2 percent is $46,478. Thus the logged and dollar results are almost identical for black poverty rates and similar for Hispanic poverty rates.

Columns 3 and 4 of Table 7 present dollar and logged regressions from the State Courts data, this time controlling for injuries (bodily versus property), case types, population density, and state fixed effects.[22] The coefficient on white poverty is negative but not statistically significant. Black poverty has a positive and statistically significant effect on awards and is larger than in the JVR data set. The coefficient on Hispanic poverty is anomalous as it switches signs to negative but is statistically insignificant at conventional levels. The Hispanic coefficient is not well-estimated across the data sets—we discuss some possible reasons for this further below. The logged awards regression in Column 4 has similar results—the coefficient on white poverty is positive but not close to statistically significant (note that in both regressions a 1 standard deviation change will switch the sign), a 1 percentage point increase in the black poverty rate raises awards by 10 percent, or approximately $50,000. Evaluated at the winning award mean of $500,000, this is smaller than the $75,000 estimate from the dollar regression by about 1 standard deviation in dollar awards. The coefficient on Hispanic poverty is smaller ($25,000 at the means) than in the dollar regression, but neither estimate is precise.

Column 5 and 6 of Table 7 analyze the Federal data both in dollar and logged form. The Federal data do not include injuries or district fixed effects, but do include case types, district population density, and year dummy variables.[23] The coefficients on white, black and Hispanic poverty rates are very similar to those found without control variables (all are within one standard deviation). Interestingly, however, the implied effects evaluated at the mean award are all larger when the regression is run in logs. The mean winning award in the Federal data is $1,169,823. Thus, evaluated at the mean, the coefficients in the logged regression suggest that increases in the white, black and Hispanic poverty rates increase awards by $48,664, $86,917, and $141,080, respectively.

What can we conclude from these regressions? Several results stand out as robust. Awards increase dramatically in areas with high black poverty rates. We estimate that a 1 percentage point increase in black poverty rates increases awards by approximately 3 percent to 10 percent on average (evaluated using either dollars or logged awards). The feasible range for forum shopping in black poverty rates is at least 10 percent, which suggests that forum shopping or careful *voir dire* could raise awards by 30 percent to 100 percent—hundreds of thousands of dollars. Increases in white poverty award rates are uniformly negative in the JVR and State Courts data, but positive in the Federal data. The Federal data set is not large and suffers from difficult problems of aggregation. Thus we would weigh the evidence from the State Courts data and especially our primary data set, the JVR data, more heavily. Our best judgment, therefore, is that increases in white poverty have a small negative effect—a 1 percentage point increase in white poverty rates is associated with perhaps a 2 percent to 3 percent reduction in awards. It should be born in mind, of course, that jury-selection procedures, court rules, and judicial oversight could act in ways to make the Federal courts operate differently vis-a-vis race and poverty than the State Courts. Thus, our conclusions apply most confidently to the State Courts.

There is some evidence that awards increase in Hispanic poverty rates even faster than in black poverty rates, perhaps by 7 percent or more, but the coefficient on Hispanic poverty rates is more variable than on black or white poverty rates and is sometimes negative, depending on the data set and functional form. In part, the problem may be due to imprecision in the term Hispanic. "Hispanic" became a distinct statistical category only in the 1980 census, and it was treated as a "race" beginning only in the Year 2000 enumeration. Until recently, Latin American immigrants were categorized as racially white and multi-ethnic. A majority of Hispanics, understood as those from Latin America, continue to choose white as their race (Etzioni 2002). In addition, usage varies across the country. In California the term Hispanic is widely rejected in favor of Latino, while Hispanic is more common in usage in Texas and Florida (the term Latino appears for the first time in the Year 2000 census). Thus, the census figures need to be adopted with caution.

Even if people of Latin American origin uniformly labeled themselves Hispanic, there is still a great deal of variation between, for example, Cuban-Americans in Miami and Mexican-Americans in Los Angeles. Our data sets cover different counties and regions and, thus, may be picking up differences in the "types" of Hispanics.[24] If this hypothesis is correct, then if we restrict the JVR data to the year and counties covered by the State Courts data,[25] and we run the same regression as in Table 7, we should expect to see a negative sign on Hispanic—this is indeed the case. On the restricted JVR data set the coefficient on Hispanic is –11,487. Although considerably smaller than in the State Courts data and not statistically significant (there are only 1,605 observations in the restricted data set), this result is suggestive that the differences between the State Courts and JVR data are due to differences in the counties covered in combination with the small size of the State Courts data. In future work we hope to break Hispanic and other populations into finer, more homogeneous categories that could be used to more precisely distinguish the effect of demographics on tort awards.

In Table 8, we focus on our largest data set and further test our earlier finding that the markup in product liability and medical-malpractice cases is much higher in high-poverty counties than in low-poverty counties. We find clear evidence that awards increase with county poverty much faster in product liability and medical-malpractice cases than in other types of cases. To further investigate this

TABLE 8 Regression of Total Award on State Fixed Effects, Injury Variables, Case Types, Population Density, and White, Black, and Hispanic Poverty—Further results JVR data.

White Poverty Rate	−9,541* (2,843)	−10,775* (2,915)
Black Poverty Rate	11,525* (5,859)	−36,002 (25,550)
Hispanic Poverty Rate	51,479* (13,588)	74,350* (25,504)
Product Liability* Black Poverty	124,093* (55,395)	
Product Liability* Hispanic Poverty	213,466* (72,823)	
Medical Malpractice* Black Poverty	36,329*** (19,977)	
Medical Malpractice* Hispanic Poverty	162,429 (64,046)	
(Black Poverty)^2		3,724** (1,863)
(Hispanic Poverty)^2		289 (2,165)
Obs.	41,150	41,150

*Significant at greater than 1% level.
**Significant at greater than 5% level.
***Significant at greater than 10% level.

effect, we test whether the increase in product and medical-liability cases is different in counties with black compared to Hispanic poverty. We find that a 1 percent increase in black or Hispanic poverty increases awards in general by about $11,000 and $51,000, respectively. In product-liability cases, however, increases in black or Hispanic poverty raise awards by an *additional* $124,000 and $213,000, respectively. In medical-malpractice cases, the additional markup is $36,000 and $162,000, respectively.[26, 27]

Figures 1 and 2 hint that the relationship between trial awards and poverty rates may be nonlinear, with the effect of poverty on awards increasing at higher rates of poverty. To test for this possibility, we square the black and Hispanic poverty rates and add these to the regression, thus allowing the relationship between black and Hispanic poverty and trial awards to increase at an increasing or decreasing rate.[28] The results, presented in Column 2, indicate that awards increase at an increasing rate in black poverty rates but at a lesser rate in Hispanic poverty rates. There is some suggestion that awards may even decrease with black poverty at low poverty rates, but the effect is very small. Figure 3 illustrates.

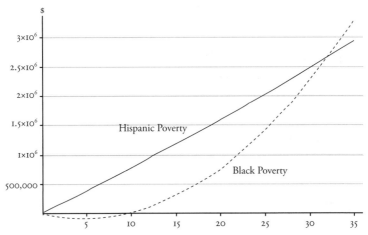

FIGURE 3 Awards Decline in Poverty Rates at Low Poverty Rates but Increase Rapidly at Higher Rates.

RACE, POVERTY AND SETTLEMENT AMOUNTS

The results indicate that trial awards increase with countywide black and Hispanic poverty rates and decrease with white poverty rates. Trials are the most visible and important output of the civil justice system.[29] Nevertheless, most disputes are settled not tried. It's worthwhile, therefore, to examine settlement data for a poverty effect.

We have data on 26,038 settlement awards from the JVR data set (neither the State Courts nor the Federal data set include data on settlement amounts). Table 9 contains results of a regression of settlement amounts on white, black and Hispanic poverty rates extracted from a regression that includes all of the control variables described above (i.e. state fixed effects, injuries, population density,

TABLE 9 Regression of Settlement Amounts on State Fixed Effects, Injury Variables, Case Types, Population Density, and White, Black, and Hispanic Poverty.

Variables	1) JVR Data	JVR-Logged Awards
White Poverty Rate	829 (2,776)	.00165 (.00202)
Black Poverty Rate	23,725* (4,994)	.01601* (.005206)
Hispanic Poverty Rate	18,106** (3,654)	.021035* (.00713)
Observations	26,038	26,038

*Significant at greater than 1% level.

**Significant at greater than 5% level.

***Significant at greater than 10% level.

Standard errors are robust (heterosecadastic-consistent).

All awards in 1996 dollars.

and case types). As we see in Column 1, Row 2, a 1 percent increase in black poverty rates increases settlement awards by nearly $24,000 while the same increase in Hispanic poverty rates increases settlement amounts by approximately $18,000 (Column 1, Row 3). When awards are logged, we estimate that a 1 percentage point increase in black poverty raises average settlement amounts by 1.6% and the same increase in Hispanic poverty raises awards by 2.1 percent (evaluated at the mean settlement award of $278,000, these are $4,450 and $5,846—somewhat smaller than the estimates from the dollar awards). The coefficient on white poverty rates is positive but small and not statistically significant.

We do not attempt to analyze how win rates, risk aversion, expected award size, the decision standard and other variables affect the relationship between settlement amounts and trial awards (see Priest and Klein 1984, Waldfogel 1995). For a back of the envelope calculation, however, assume that the settlement award is based on the expected trial award. Using an average win rate of 50 percent, the above increase in settlement amount with black and Hispanic poverty rates translates into increases in awards conditional on winning of $44,000 and $36,000, respectively, or (using the log estimates) 3.2

percent and 4.1 percent, respectively. These effects are consistent with those found in the trial award equations.

We have also examined win rates and settlement rates, but in all cases the effect of the various poverty rates was negligible.[30] For example, we found a 10 percent increase in black poverty was responsible for a 0.0408 percent point increase in the probability of winning a case (i.e. plus 0.0408 units in the probability of winning). Other results were on the same order (results are available upon request). Thus we find that the main effects of poverty rates occur on awards.

The lack of an effect on win rates is not surprising because the cases that go to trial tend to be coin-toss cases, that is, cases with a lot of uncertainty in win rates (Priest and Klein 1984). If the plaintiff and defendant can easily predict the outcome of the case, the case will settle because of the potential savings in trial costs. An exogenous change might increase win rates temporarily, but as expectations adjust, more cases will be settled leaving, once again, the most uncertain cases to go to trial. Under some conditions, trial win rates will always approach 50 percent. Although case selection makes the interpretation of win rates quite difficult, this phenomenon is less true of awards. In the standard Priest-Klein model, for example, the distribution of awards is not at all affected by case selection.[31] A proper test of the effect of poverty on win rates requires information on the trial rate. It is possible to create a trial rate from the Federal data and, thus, a potential test is available following the methods in Waldfogel (1995). We leave such a test to future research.

CONCLUSIONS

The results indicate that awards fall with white poverty levels (or increase only moderately in the Federal data), but increase dramatically with black poverty rates. Awards also appear to increase with Hispanic poverty rates; although, the results are more variable. An increase in the black poverty rate of 1 percentage point tends to raise the average personal-injury tort award by 3 percent to 10 percent ($20,000 to $60,000), and our best estimate is that an increase in the Hispanic poverty rate of 1 percentage point tends to raise awards by 7 percent. Yet awards tend to fall by 2 percent to 3 percent for every 1 percentage point increase in white poverty rates. A fall in awards is to be expected if compensatory awards fall with lower wages, thus the increase in awards with black and Hispanic poverty is especially surprising. Since the variation in county poverty rates is large, "forum shopping," or moving a trial from a low-poverty county to a high-poverty county, can substantially increase the average award.

Awards increase with black and Hispanic poverty rates even after controlling for a wide variety of other potential causes including injuries, population densities, case types, any factors, such as legal differences, associated with states and any factor correlated with white poverty rates. Settlement amounts also increase with increases in black and Hispanic county poverty rates. It is unlikely that the difference in awards can be explained by any factors specific to the case or to differences in law. It appears that socioeconomic factors can exert large effects on awards, thus calling into question a typical assumption of "law and economics" type reasoning.

One hypothesis that could explain our results is that poor black and Hispanic jurors decide cases differently than white jurors of all economic levels. Given the different life experiences of poor black and Hispanic jury members relative to whites of all economic levels, it appears plausible that the decisions of such jurors about justice and due compensation could differ significantly from those of other jurors. Such a finding is also consistent with anecdotal evidence and with the literature on race differences in decision-making concerning criminal trials.

Runaway Judges?
Selection Effects and the Jury

Are juries out of control? In Chapter 2, we demonstrated that tort awards increase dramatically with county poverty rates. Other researchers and pundits have charged that juries are biased in favor of the plaintiff, tend to be guided by emotion rather than by reason, have a poor understanding of the law and are wildly unpredictable. Anecdotal evidence of jury bias is found regularly in the popular press. A complaint made by the North Carolina Hospital Association (1986) is typical of how the issue is viewed:

> Often awards have little relationship to the seriousness of injury. There is no way to predict how a jury will rule on a particular set of facts.... Often awards bear no relationship to economic losses ... today juries often make awards regardless of the 'fault' of anyone—out of sympathy for an injured person ... too often juries appear to award on [the] basis of emotion as opposed to facts and/or realistic evaluation of case circumstances.[1]

David Bernstein (1996), a law professor who has studied the tort reforms of several countries, agrees with these allegations, calling juries "a disaster for the civil justice system" because they "undermine certainty, are incompetent to decide complex cases, and often base their decisions on illegitimate factors." In Australia, Canada, and England, Bernstein notes pointedly, "judges alone handle personal injury cases." Bernstein and others argue that judges are better than juries at evaluating complicated evidence (a factor in many medical malpractice and product-liability trials), are less likely to be swayed by emotion, and are more likely to closely follow the principles of tort law (see also Tullock 1998). Tort reforms, therefore, typically try to limit the jury's discretion by capping the amounts that juries may award for pain and suffering, to give one example. More generally, opponents of the current tort system argue that when compared with the rest of the world, the American reliance on the jury is anachronistic and should be curtailed.[2]

Critics of the tort system are not alone in their perception of significant differences in the quality of the decisions made by juries and those made by judges. As a practitioners' handbook on trial law suggests: "As a general rule, most plaintiffs with highly charged cases want a jury in the hope that the jury will be swept away in a tide of emotion and award large damages" (Izard 1998). Juries are also said to be preferable for plaintiffs when the case does not rest on complex facts or legal technicalities and when the plaintiff is a "little guy" relative to the defendant.[3]

Such advice to plaintiff lawyers certainly is suggestive, but what systematic evidence do we have that judges will decide cases differently than juries?

JUDGES VERSUS JURIES

Surprisingly, the academic literature on judges versus juries does *not* find large differences in their decision-making. In their classic study, *The American Jury*, Kalven and Zeisel (1966) surveyed the judges who presided over some 4,000 civil *jury* trials. In 78 percent of the trials, the presiding judges would have ruled the same as the juries had it been up to them. This rate of agreement is comparable to the rate of agreement among different experts of all kinds (for example, scientists reviewing the research of peers, physicians diagnosing patients, etc.), and importantly, it is comparable to the rate of agreement among different judges (Diamond 1983).[4] When Kalven and Zeisel found disagreement among judge and jury, it was almost as likely that the judge found liability and the jury did not as in the reverse case.[5]

Most of the studies of judge/jury differences rely on hypothetical questions—judges are asked what they would have done *if* they had been responsible for deciding the case—or they rely on artificial experiments. Almost no research on judge/jury differences has been done using nonsurvey data on judge and jury outcomes.

The first systematic effort to look at this question using litigation data was by Clermont and Eisenberg (1992). They compared win rates and awards in a sample of federal civil trials and found that win rates often differ significantly across the trial forum and not always in ways predicted by the critics of the jury system; in some types of cases, plaintiff win rates are higher in judge trials than in jury trials. Clermont and Eisenberg primarily were interested in explaining why judge trials are more prevalent in some areas of litigation than in other areas. In particular, they focused on the puzzle of why plaintiffs predominantly choose jury trials, even in case categories where judge win rates are significantly higher than jury win rates. They suggested that a combination of selection effects and misperceptions might explain the data. We also offer some comments on this issue further below.

MEAN AWARDS AND WIN RATES

To test whether judges and juries decide cases similarly, we used a large data set that includes data on settlements as well as on trial outcomes. The data was extracted from Jury Verdict Research's *Personal Injury Verdicts and Settlements* on CD-ROM. (The sample is similar to that discussed in Chapter 2.)

Table 1 presents data on win rates, mean, and median awards, the log standard deviation of awards, and the number of trials in each category (Table 1 does not include data on settlements). At first glance, the table appears to support the claims of jury reformers that the jury is biased towards the plaintiff. The mean award in a case before a jury is more than twice as large as the mean award in a case before a judge. Contrary to the conventional wisdom, however, the win rate before judges is significantly higher than the win rate before juries. The higher judge win rate, however, does not fully offset the larger awards given by juries—the expected award given by juries is larger than the expected award given by judges.

The median award given by a jury is significantly larger than the median judge award. Thus, the larger jury mean award is not simply an artifact of the occasional astronomical award given by a jury. In both judge and jury cases, the mean award is significantly larger than the median award, which suggests a strongly right-skewed distribution. Figure 1 graphs the distribution of log awards.[6] The graph of jury awards clearly has a larger mean and standard deviation than that for judge awards. Aside from the higher win rate in judge trials, the raw data appears to support the case for jury reform.

THE IMPORTANCE OF SAMPLE SELECTION

SAMPLE SELECTION AND AWARDS

The average judge award is only 31 percent of the average jury award. Judges and juries, however, may see different types of cases. If this is true, then awards could be different even if judges and juries would decide the same cases identically. How much of the difference in awards can be explained by differences in the types of cases appearing before judges and juries? To answer this question, we control for possible differences in: (1) case categories (perhaps, for example,

TABLE I Judge/Jury differences (all trials).

	Juries	Judges	Two Sided *p*-Value on Difference[C]
Win Rate	56.67%	67.73%	0.000
Mean Award[A]	$696,149	$218,629	0.000
Median Award[A]	$74,879	$17,279	0.000
Mean of Log Awards	11.24	10.02	0.000
Standard Deviation of Log Awards	2.188	1.853	0.000
(Dollar Equivalent)[A, B]	($603,156)	($121,885)	
Number of Trials	53,335	5,969	

[A] Conditional on a plaintiff win.

[B] Since dollar awards are not normally distributed, the standard deviation of dollar awards is not informative. The standard deviation of log awards has meaning, however, because log awards are well approximated by a normal distribution. To convert a standard deviation in logs back to a dollar figure, we evaluate at the mean of the log awards.

[C] The *p*-values for the difference in win rates, means, and standard deviations give the probability that the sample difference would have been as large or larger than that estimated if there were no difference in the true means. The *p*-values are two-sided and were computed using standard tests available in any text (e.g., Aczel, 1996). The difference in medians test was computed using a Monte-Carlo method with 5,000 replications.

Source: JVR

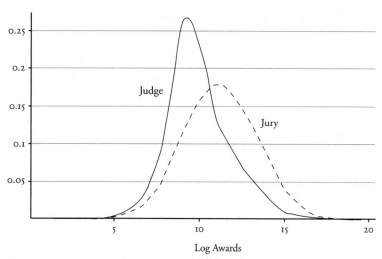

FIGURE I Kernal Densities, All Cases: Judge and Jury.

judges see more auto cases and fewer product-liability cases) (2) injuries and other variables (perhaps judges see fewer cases involving deaths) and (3) unobserved factors that are correlated with the plaintiff's or defendant's decision to opt for a jury trial (even if we aren't sure what the differences are, there are some statistical techniques that let us control for them—see further below).

It's well-known that awards in product liability and medical-malpractice cases are much larger than in premises liability and auto-injury cases.[7] Column 1 of Table 2, for example, shows a regression of log awards (in jury trials) on these four case categories.[8] Evaluated at the mean log award, awards are approximately $180,000 and $187,000 larger than average in product liability and medical-malpractice cases, and $25,000 and $100,000 lower than average in premises liability and auto cases, respectively.

Product-liability cases and medical-malpractice cases are comparatively rare; they make up 4.7 percent and 7.3 percent of jury trials, respectively. Premises liability and auto-injury cases are much more common, these case categories account for 15.2 percent and 47.5 percent of our sample of jury trials. (Descriptive statistics on all variables can be found in Table A1 in Appendix A.)

If product liability and medical-malpractice cases are proportionately a larger part of the jury sample than the judge sample, this could explain why the average jury award is so much larger than the average judge award. In fact, this is the situation: The high-award case types, product liability and medical malpractice, make up only 1.51 percent and 1.58 percent of judge trials, respectively, while the low-award types, premises liability and auto-accident cases, account for 9 percent and 64.9 percent of the judge sample.

To establish the importance of this source of variation, we ask: "If juries had decided the cases that actually went to judges, how much lower would the average award have been?"[9] Using the coefficients from Table 2, we find that if juries had decided the sample of cases going to judges, the average award in that sample would have been

TABLE 2 Award Regressions on Jury Trials (no correction for sample selection).

	OLS Jury	OLS Jury
Constant	11.747*** (.023)	11.61*** (.069)
Number of Defendants		.423*** (.051)
Expected Years of Life Left		.272*** (.02)
Major Injury		.633*** (.071)
Minor Injury		−.995*** (.065)
Emotional Distress		−1.16*** (.0769)
Bad Faith		−.134 (.113)
Male		.327*** (.218)
Premises Liability	−.386*** (.038)	−.101*** (.037)
Medical Malpractice	1.311*** (.049)	.815*** (.47)
Product Liability	1.255*** (.0579)	.652*** (.055)
Auto	−1.27*** (.0285)	−.915*** (.0299)
Poverty		2.22*** (.197)
Joint and Several Liability		.091* (.049)
Non-Economic Cap		−.528*** (.028)
Collateral Sources		.322*** (.218)
No Punitive		−.081 (.129)
Punitive Cap		−.106 (.022)
Evidence Standard		.18*** (.024)
Number of Cases	30,226	30,226

*Significant at greater than .1% level.
**Significant at greater than .05% level.
***Significant at greater than .01% level.
Standard Errors in parentheses.

63 percent of the average jury award. Thus, just over half of the difference in average judge and jury awards can be explained solely by differences in the sample of four case-categories going to judge and jury trial.[10]

We now add injuries, differences in tort law across the states, the number of defendants, and local poverty rates to the list of variables that may lead to different judge/jury samples. Our data set has descriptive information on the victim's injury. We code this information into six variables. Five of the variables, Major Injury, Minor Injury, Emotional Distress, Bad Faith, and Wrongful Termination, are dummy variables. Major is set equal to one if the victim suffered a permanent injury such as loss of limb, brain damage, or blindness. Minor injuries are those that are (potentially) temporary, for example, broken arms, broken legs, concussions, or wounds. A pianist might consider a broken finger a major injury if recovery was not 100 percent complete. We do not know all of the specifics of a case, so we cannot control for potential miscodings of this type; nevertheless, any coding errors will be uncorrelated with our other independent variables. Emotional Distress indicates cases in which the victim suffered emotional or psychological injuries. Bad Faith cases are those in which an insurance company is sued for refusing to pay a claim. Wrongful Termination is set equal to one when the plaintiff claims a wrongful termination of employment.[11] We also include a sixth variable, the expected years of life left in a case in which the victim died. We calculated the expected years of life left using the age at death and actuarial tables that control for age and sex. We do not have data on lost wages, but we do include a dummy variable set equal to one when the victim was a male on the theory that average wage losses are higher for males than females. Together these variables control for the severity of a plaintiff's injury.

In addition to injuries, we include a number of legal variables that may affect liability. Under the joint and several rule, any defendant can be liable for a plaintiff's entire injury regardless of the relative contribution of that defendant to the injury. Most states have modified the joint and several rule to limit the liability of some defendants (for example, a defendant responsible for less than 50 percent of the injury may not be assessed more than his relative contribution). Joint and several is set equal to one if the state has modified the rule and if there is more than one defendant. Noneconomic Cap is set equal to one if state law puts a cap on damages due to pain and suffering or other noneconomic losses. Punitive Cap and No Punitive control for states that cap punitive awards or prohibit them altogether.[12] Evidence standard is set equal to one if the state requires that "malicious intent" be *proven* for punitive damages to be recoverable. Under the collateral sources rule, payments to the plaintiff from a third party (i.e., insurance) are not deducted from damages due from the defendant. If collateral sources is set equal to one, the collateral sources rule is weakened so that some offset is allowed.[13]

The variable Poverty measures the percentage of the population in poverty in the county in which the trial occurs. The number of defendants is included as another control variable that may affect the size of awards. The descriptive statistics for the independent variables are given in Appendix A1.

Column 2 of Table 2 shows the impact of these variables on awards. As before, awards are higher than average in product liability and medical-malpractice trials and lower than average in premises liability and auto trials. Also, as expected, awards are higher than average in cases involving deaths and major injuries and lower than average in cases involving minor injuries, emotional distress, or bad-faith contracting. Limitations on joint and several awards tend to raise awards, a result the opposite of that expected, but the effect is small and not statistically significant at the 5 percent level. Caps on noneconomic awards and punitive awards appear to reduce awards as intended. In both cases, the effect is highly statistically significant. Evidence standards, however, do not appear to lower awards. Awards also tend to be larger in states where the collateral sources rule is weakened (allowing defendants to introduce evidence that the plaintiff will recover from other sources such as insurance), perhaps because juries top up awards if they think insurance payments will later be deducted.[14] Trials with multiple defendants appear to generate larger awards than otherwise similar trials.[15] Finally, the higher the poverty rate of the county in which the trial occurs (the jury pool), the greater the award.[16] (We look at marginal effects in more detail further below).

If trials before judges tend to involve fewer deaths or major injuries than trials before juries, or if they tend to occur in richer counties or in states which cap pain and suffering awards, then differences in the sample could explain differences in the average award. Taking into account all of these possible sources of variation, we find that if the judge sample had been tried before a jury, the average award in the judge sample would have been 56 percent lower than the average jury award. Case-type variables alone already suggested that the average award in the judge sample would be 63 percent lower than the jury average. Injuries, differences in tort law, the number of defendants, and local poverty rates do not, therefore, greatly increase our ability to explain the difference in judge and jury average awards.[17] Using case types and all of the additional variables, we are able to explain approximately 64 percent of the difference in average awards, $(100-56)/(100-31) = .638$.

SAMPLE SELECTION AND THE ESTIMATION PROCEDURE

To be awarded damages before a jury, at least one of the defendants or the plaintiff must have requested a jury trial, the case must not have been settled, and the plaintiff must have won at trial. We have controlled for some differences in the samples, but the multiple sources of selection suggest that there may be other unobserved factors that both cause a case to be selected and influence awards. If these factors differ across judges and juries, they could also explain some of the differences in awards. To account for this sample selection, we estimate models for the forum, settlement, and win decisions, and then use Heckman's (1979) procedure to control for any correlation of errors between each of these decision equations and the award equation. We pass over most of the results from this procedure here, but details can be found in Helland and Tabarrok (2000). We focus on the comparison between judges and juries.

COMPARING THE DECISION PROCESS OF JUDGES AND JURIES

AWARDS

Table 3 contains award regressions for judges and juries controlling for sample selection. In Column 3, we give F tests of the difference in coefficient values across the two equations. The F tests indicate that there are systematic differences between judges and juries in the impact that various factors have on awards. Bearing in mind that the judge equation is not as well-estimated as the jury equation and that some of the coefficient values in the judge equation appear implausible, we can gain some insights by comparing the judge and jury coefficients.

Juries appear to be more sympathetic to injured plaintiffs than are judges. Holding the sample constant, juries give larger awards than judges for every injury category with the exception of Expected Years of Life Left, for which no significant judge/jury differences are found.

Caps on damages for pain and suffering (Noneconomic Caps) cause a greater decline in awards when the case is decided by a jury than when the case is decided by a judge. The greater effectiveness of caps on juries is also consistent with the evidence on injuries discussed above. If juries grant larger awards than judges for pain and suffering when they are allowed to do so, it follows that juries rather than judges will be constrained by caps. Since judges grant fewer large pain and suffering awards to begin with, we find that caps on judges are "less effective" because they are less necessary. The collateral resources rule also has a different impact on jury than on judges; it increases the award in jury trials, but has no effect on trials before a judge. Again, this effect is consistent with a story in which juries neutralize a weakening of the collateral sources rule by topping awards up while judges, perhaps out of greater respect for the law, do not try to offset the law's intended effect.

TABLE 3 Award Regressions for Jury and Judge (with correction for sample selection).

	3-level Jury	3-level Judge	F-test
Constant	10.96*** (1.15)	15.72*** (3.19)	1.96
Number of Defendants	.66*** (.0606)	.666*** (.162)	.001
Expected Years of Life Left	.35** (.026)	.322 (.275)	.0009
Major Injury	.862*** (.0792)	−.58* (.34)	16.44***
Minor Injury	−.926*** (.0715)	−1.65*** (.324)	4.8**
Emotional Distress	−1.06*** (.0843)	−1.92*** (.354)	5.49**
Bad Faith	−.013 (.123)	−.966* (.518)	3.37*
Male	.325*** (.024)	.157** (.08)	4.05**
Premises Liability	−.726** (.289)	−.079 (1.3)	.361
Medical Malpractice	−.693 (.681)	1.89 (3.38)	.563
Product Liability	−.112 (.327)	1.03 (1.78)	.398
Auto	−.336* (.193)	−.555 (1.71)	.016
Poverty	3.03*** (.233)	−2.64*** (.86)	40.15***
Joint and Several Liability	−.055 (.0568)	−.02 (.16)	.198
Noneconomic Cap	−.479*** (.032)	−.189* (.113)	6.04**
Collateral Sources	.250*** (.024)	.0042 (.118)	4.14**
No Punitive	−.152 (.144)	.186 (.586)	.315
Punitive Cap	−.146*** (.024)	−.07 (.084)	.749
Evidence Standard	.106*** (.027)	.173 (.116)	.313
IMR Trial Mode	−1.00*** (.172)	.399 (.258)	20.3***
IMR Settle	−.866*** (.0623)	−1.73*** (.228)	13.5***
IMR Win	3.41** (1.75)	−1.53 (5.33)	.779
Number of Cases	30,226	4,043	34,269

* Significant at the greater than .1 level
** Significant at the greater than .05 level
*** Significant at the greater than .01 level
Correct Standard Errors in parentheses—see text.

The most robust difference between judges and juries arises in the impact of local poverty. An increase in the local poverty rate raises jury awards significantly—just as we expected from the results of Chapter 2. But when judges decide cases, awards fall in local poverty rates! A 1 standard deviation increase in the local poverty rate causes a slight reduction in judge awards of $3,394 (evaluated at the means).

The fact that jury awards increase in poverty rates but judge awards fall is strong evidence in favor of our hypothesis that the local poverty effect is caused by jury composition.

The influence of local poverty on juries is the most important explanation for the "unexplained" difference in average awards discussed above. If poverty had no affect on juries (i.e., if the coefficient on poverty in the jury equation were zero, then we could have explained 100 percent of the difference in average awards on the basis of sample differences). In other words, if poverty had no influence on jury awards, juries would have given the same average award to the judge sample of cases as judges actually gave.

WIN RATES—SAMPLE SELECTION OR
DIFFERENCES IN DECISION PROCESSES?

So far we have focused on differences in awards, but there are also differences in win rates across judges and juries. The average win rate in a jury case is 56.67 percent and in a judge case is 67.73 percent. As with awards, however, some of this difference is due to a different sample of cases rather than to differences in decisions. Using the coefficients for the jury win equation in Table 4, we can estimate what the win rate would have been if the sample of cases going to judges had instead been decided by juries—60.04 percent. Sample selection can thus explain about 30 percent of the difference in judge and jury win rates $(60.04-56.67)/(67.73-56.67)=.3$.

Since most of the difference in win rates appears not to be caused by sample selection, there may be significant differences in win decision processes across judges and juries. Using a likelihood ratio (LR) test, given in the final column, we can compare the coefficients from the jury and judge win. The test rejects at the 10 percent level or greater the null hypothesis of identical judge and jury win coefficients for every variable except products defense and the constant.

Marginal effects from the jury and judge win equations are presented in Table 5. Significantly almost all of the marginal effects run
in the *opposite* direction to that of the average win rate. The average
win rate is higher for judges than for juries, but this is almost entirely
due to the higher win rate of auto cases before judges than before
juries. Consistent with the anecdotal evidence, plaintiffs with product liability and medical-malpractice cases are more likely to win
before juries than before judges (although these cases are harder to
win than the average in both forums).

TABLE 4 The Win Decision: Jury versus Judge.

Variable	Jury Win Probit	Judge Win Probit	LR-test χ^2
Constant	.227*** (.011)	.283*** (.033)	2.54
Expected Years of Life Left if Defendant Died	.0025 (.006)	−.089*** (.019)	18.879***
Product Liability	−.231*** (.034)	−.5** (.128)	4.18*
Medical Malpractice	−.595*** (.02)	−.936*** (.093)	13.26***
Auto	.19*** (.014)	.66*** (.042)	114.55***
Premises Liability	−.265*** (.017)	−.399*** (.054)	5.656**
Joint and Several Liability No limit on contingency fees Products Defense	−.125*** (.046)	−.045 (.207)	.141
Number of Cases	53,335	5,969	

TABLE 5 Marginal Effects, Judge and Jury Win Equations.

	Jury	Judge
Expected Years of Life Left	−.09%	−3.1%
Product Liability	−9.1%	−19.7%
Medical Malpractice	−23.3%	−35.5%
Auto	7.4%	23.1%
Premises Liability	−10.5%	−14.8%
Product Defense	−4.9%	−1.5%

DISCUSSION

Bernstein (1996) argues that in an ideal world juries would be eliminated for civil trials. "Unfortunately," he continues, this would be unconstitutional in most states. As a result, the most "important measure that legislatures can take to eliminate the pernicious effects of civil juries is to remove the issue of damages from the jury and put it in the hands of judges." Our results show that such a reform would have a smaller effect on awards than Bernstein and other tort reformers imagine.

There is some truth, however, to the views of the tort reformers. Juries do grant systematically larger awards to injured plaintiffs than judges. Juries also appear to be more receptive to "redistribute the wealth" arguments than judges. In particular, juries drawn from pools with high-poverty rates grant systematically larger awards than do judges and juries drawn from more affluent regions. Win rates in product-liability and medical-malpractice cases are higher before juries than judges. The differences in judge and jury decision-making we have discovered, however, explain only a quarter to a one-third of the difference in average award rates across judges and juries. Three-quarters to two-thirds of the difference in average awards is due not to differences in decision-making, but to differences in the sample of cases appearing before judges and juries. The difference in average awards across judge and juries gives a very misleading picture of what would happen if the United States followed the rest of the world and shifted decision-making from the judge to the jury.

Tort reformers often point the finger of blame for high awards on juries, but the revolution in product liability and medical-malpractice law that has occurred over the past forty years has been a product not of juries but of judges (Priest 1991, Epstein 1980). If juries have granted large awards in class-action suits, it is the judges who have rewritten the law to enable those suits to be brought, often on the flimsiest of evidence. From this perspective, it's not surprising that judges grant similar awards to juries—the judges are leading the charge.

APPENDIX

TABLE A1 Descriptive Statistics.

Variable	Mean	Std. Dev.
Jury Trial Awards		
Log(Jury Award)	11.24	2.187
Number of Defendants	.2336	.4055
Expected Years of Life Left	.2433	.9215
Major Injury	.1132	.3169
Minor Injury	.7268	.4456
Emotional Distress	.05102	.22
Bad Faith	.0126	.1117
Male	.51	.5
Premises Liability	.152	.3591
Medical Malpractice	.0729	.26
Product Liability	.04744	.2126
Auto	.4752	.4994
Poverty	.1281	.05512
Joint and Several Liability	.2366	.42499
Non-Economic Cap	.1908	.3929
Collateral Sources	.4983	.5
No Punitive	.0711	.08404
Punitive Cap	.52	.4996
Evidence Standard	.322	.4674
Judge Trial Awards		
Log (Judge Award)	10.027	1.853
Number of Defendants	.245	.41094
Expected Years of Life Left	.156	.77
Major Injury	.121	.326
Minor Injury	.766	.4237
Emotional Distress	.0493	.2164
Bad Faith	.0866	.09268
Male	.48	.5
Premises Liability	.0933	.2909
Medical Malpractice	.0151	.122
Product Liability	.0158	.125
Auto	.649	.4773
Poverty	.138	.0583
Joint and Several Liability	.203	.4022
Non-Economic Cap	.231	.421
Collateral Sources	.273	.446
No Punitive	.0047	.0684
Punitive Cap	.606	.489
Evidence Standard	.262	.4396

TABLE A1 Descriptive Statistics. (*cont.*)

Variable	Mean	Std. Dev.
Forum Choice		
Forum Choice (Jury=1)	.899	.3008
Auto	.4197	.4935
Number of Defendants	.2332	.4092
Time Difference	1.009	.2321
Default (1=Judge)	.229	.4204
Plaintiff Request	.455	.659
Defendant Request	.662	.792
Trial Equation		
Does the case go to trial (yes=1)	.683	.465
Product Liability	.0474	.212
Medical Malpractice	.0955	.294
Expected Time to Trial	6.663	.157
Number of Defendants	.239	.4153
Child	.434	.496
Expected Years of Life Left	.288	1.003
Joint and Several Liability	.225	.417
No limit on contingency fees	.47	.499
Jury Win Equation		
Plaintiff win at a jury trial(yes=1)	.567	.4955
Product Liability	.057	.2315
Auto	.407	.4913
Medical Malpractice	.116	.3203
Premises liability	.178	.3822
Expected Years of Life Left	.2705	.9663
Products Defense	.0287	.1671
Judge Win Equation		
Plaintiff win at a judge trial(yes=1)	.677	.468
Product Liability	.028	.165
Auto	.534	.499
Medical Malpractice	.0426	.202
Premises liability	.141	.348
Expected Years of Life Left	.2171	.906
Products Defense	.01	.0998

TABLE A2 Time to Trial Results.

	Logistic Hazard Model Judge	Logistic Hazard Model Jury
Constant	7.15***	5.109***
	(.419)	(.273)
Death	.133***	.073
	(.023)	(.154)
Major Injury	.143	−.245*
	(.213)	(.135)
Minor Injury	.03	−.14
	(.02)	(.126)
Emotional Distress	−.097	−.153
	(.023)	(.146)
Premises Liability	−.005	.204***
	(.104)	(.077)
Medical Malpractice	.211***	.292**
	(.119)	(.124)
Product Liability	.212***	.327**
	(.016)	(.14)
Log(number of defendants)	.046***	.173***
	(.004)	(.026)
Auto	−.164***	−.42***
	(.009)	(.054)
Number of cases filled per judge in the state	−.067***	.1**
	(.005)	(.034)
Number of Cases	36896	5496

* Significant at the greater than .01 level

** Significant at the greater than .05 level

*** Significant at the greater than .01 level

Asymptotic Standard Errors in parentheses

4

The Effect of Judicial Elections on Tort Awards

In the previous chapter, we showed that there is some truth to the conventional wisdom that juries are more generous to injured plaintiffs than are judges. Juries also appear to be swayed more than judges by appeals to redistribute the wealth as we saw in both Chapters 2 and 3. The differences between juries and judges, however, should not be exaggerated—if juries and judges were given *the same cases*, the average judge award would be modestly lower than the average jury award, but not overwhelmingly so. We should not forget that the expansion in tort law has been driven by judges more than by juries.

In this chapter, we focus on judges and their incentive structure. In particular, we ask: What difference does the electoral system have on judicial incentives and tort awards? State court judges are elected in twenty-three states and are appointed in twenty-seven. Of the twenty-three states in which judges are elected, ten of them use highly competitive partisan elections while in the remainder judges run on nonpartisan ballots. Federal judges are appointed and have life tenure while, as noted above, many state court judges are elected and, with the exception of Superior Court judges in Rhode Island, none have life tenure. In this chapter, we argue that in cases involving corporate defendants with out-of-state headquarters, elected judges, particularly partisan-elected judges, have an incentive to grant larger awards than other judges. We test the partisan-election hypothesis using both of the divisions discussed above.

We first test the partisan-election hypothesis by comparing cases in partisan-elected states with cases in states using other selection mechanisms. We control for other influences that might differ across the states. One difference across the states, which appears difficult to control for, is that each state has its own body of tort law. It might be thought that the effect of selection mechanisms cannot be distinguished from the effect of tort law because, for example, only Alabama judges apply Alabama law. We take advantage of a peculiar aspect of American federalism to make this distinction. In cases involving citizens of different states, aptly called "diversity-of-citizenship" cases, *federal judges apply state law* to decide disputes. Diversity-of-citizenship cases, therefore, provide an ideal natural experiment. Do appointed and politically insulated federal judges make the same decisions as elected state judges when both apply the same law?

THE PARTISAN-ELECTION HYPOTHESIS

The dominant methods of judicial selection are partisan elections, nonpartisan elections, gubernatorial appointment, legislative election, and merit plans. The "merit plan," however, is gubernatorial appointment from a slate of candidates put forward by a nominating commission. Furthermore, the governor typically appoints at least some members of the nominating commission. The governor also plays an important role in legislative election, which is used in only three states (Connecticut, South Carolina, and Virginia). The main categories are thus partisan elections, nonpartisan elections, and appointment systems.

Elected judges must cater to the demands of the voters, and they must seek campaign funds from interested parties. Appointed judges, by contrast, do not answer to the voters in competitive elections nor do they need to raise significant campaign funds. Furthermore, appointed judges tend to have longer terms than elected judges, on average 21 percent to 27 percent longer for general and supreme courts, respectively (Hanssen 1999). Appointed judges are also more secure than elected judges; they are returned to the bench—through reappointment or a retention election—more often than are elected judges.[1] Appointed judges are thus more insulated from direct political pressure than are elected judges and will tend to be more independent (Hanssen 1999; Posner 1993, p. 41; and Dubois 1990).

In a partisan-election state, judges run under a party banner, just as do other politicians. In a nonpartisan election state, judges do not run under banners and are required by law to be independent of party. Elections tend to be more competitive in partisan than in nonpartisan states. Although judicial elections in nonpartisan states are more competitive than retention elections, they are still not very competitive. Many judges run unopposed, and when they are opposed, few incumbents are defeated. Partisan elections tend to be contested more often and, as a result, voter turnout is higher and incumbents are defeated more regularly than in nonpartisan elections (Dubois 1979, Glick 1983). Of elected states, ten use partisan elections.[2]

PREVIOUS RESEARCH INTO JUDICIAL ELECTORAL SYSTEMS

Judicial selection mechanisms are the subject of a large literature in political science, law, and judicial studies. The dominant approach in these studies has been sociological. The sociological approach posits that judicial outcomes are a function of judicial characteristics such as race, sex, education, and wealth. According to this view, if selection mechanisms have an effect on outcomes, they must do so by selecting for different types of judges. A large literature has tested whether judicial elections or appointments bring more minorities, women, conservatives, and so on to the bench or whether the American Bar Association ratings of appointed judges are higher or lower than those of elected judges. Almost unanimously, this literature concludes that selection mechanisms have no significant effects on any judicial characteristics (see, for example, Flango and Ducat 1979; Glick and Emmert 1987; Alozie 1990; and the reviews of the literature in Baum 1995; and Stumpf and Culver 1992). Unlike the sociological approach, we hypothesize that selection mechanisms affect outcomes through incentives even if they have little or no effect on measurable judicial characteristics.[3] Our hypothesis is thus framed and tested directly in terms of outcomes—in our case, awards in personal injury cases.

In Tabarrok and Helland (1999), we used a sample of 7,642 trial awards to compare awards in partisan-elected states, nonpartisan elected states, and nonelected states. We found that the average award in a case involving an out-of-state defendant was much higher in partisan-elected states than in nonpartisan elected states or nonelected states. Furthermore, we could not reject the hypothesis that awards were the same in nonpartisan elected states and nonelected states. We thus concentrate on the difference in awards between partisan-elected states and other selection systems, which we call nonpartisan systems.

In this chapter, we take advantage of a peculiar aspect American federalism to test the partisan-election hypothesis. If a citizen of Texas sues a citizen of Oklahoma, both citizens have the option of having the case heard in federal court (limitations are described in greater detail below). In these diversity-of-citizenship cases, federal judges decide disputes on the basis of state law. Since federal judges are unelected and have life tenure, we expect significant differences between awards in cases decided by federal judges and awards in cases decided by state court judges, even when the federal judges apply state law. We discuss diversity of citizenship cases and our test procedure at greater length below.

Most cases are settled rather than tried, and tried cases represent a nonrandom selection of disputes. To find the true effect of partisan elections on awards, we use a large data set of 52,545 observations of trial awards and 22,455 observations of settlements to control for any differences in the types of disputes that go to trial in partisan and nonpartisan states.[4] We also control for any differences in the winning disputes in partisan versus nonpartisan states.

WHY MIGHT SELECTION MECHANISMS MATTER?

Here we outline three theories for why judicial selection mechanisms might have an effect on trial awards. Elections may cause judges to curry the favor of plaintiffs, who more often are voters than are defendants; they may cause judges to seek campaign contributions from lawyers interested in larger awards; and elections may increase judicial diversity in ways that increase the mean award. The theories are not necessarily mutually exclusive. Our goal in this chapter is to show that the method by which judges are elected has a large and statistically significant impact on tort awards, rather than to pinpoint the exact cause of this impact.

Judges in elected states must cater to the demands of voters. Plaintiffs typically sue in the state in which they live, so most plaintiffs are voters. Defendants, however, are often corporations headquartered in other states or even other countries.[5] Plaintiffs, therefore, will tend to be more politically powerful than out-of-state defendants, especially in states with elected judiciaries. Richard Neely, a retired West Virginia Supreme Court judge, made this point frankly:

> As long as I am allowed to redistribute wealth from out-of-state companies to injured in-state plaintiffs, I shall continue to do so. Not only is my sleep enhanced when I give someone else's money away, but so is my job security, because the in-state plaintiffs, their families, and their friends will reelect me (Neely 1988, p. 4).

Furthermore, Neely continues, "It should be obvious that the in-state local plaintiff, his witnesses, and his friends, can all vote for the judge, while the out-of-state defendant can't even be relied upon to send a campaign donation" (Neely 1988, p. 62). Redistributing wealth from out-of-state defendants to in-state plaintiffs is a judge's way of providing constituency service.[6,7] Maloney, McCormick, and Tollison (1984) make the same argument with respect to government regulators. They argue that a vote-maximizing regulator will transfer wealth from out-of-state consumers to in-state consumers by raising prices whenever out-of-state consumers consume a large fraction of industry output. Applying the theory to electricity prices, they find that a 10 percent increase in electricity exports raises the price of electricity by 4.5 percent.

A second explanation for the partisan-electoral effect focuses on interest groups and campaign contributions. Just like politicians in the legislative branches of government, elected judges must raise significant amounts of campaign funds in order be elected and reelected. In the aggregate, campaign funds may not bias politicians much one way or the other. For every politician who accepts campaign contributions from big business, it is plausible that there is another who accepts funds from labor unions. The need for campaign funds, however, is more likely to bias the judiciary in deciding awards in tort cases. The judiciary affects interest groups from across the political spectrum, but the interest groups don't know which of the thousands of judges will rule in their particular case. (And once a judge has been assigned to a case, it is usually too late to engage in effective lobbying.) A pharmaceutical company, for example, has an interest in liability law, but it doesn't know when or where it might be sued, let alone be familiar with the judge who will preside over the case. The random assignment of judges to cases means that the most consistent contributors to judicial campaigns are trial lawyers.

Unlike other participants, trial lawyers engage in repeated interactions with the same judges and so have the most incentive to make campaign contributions. Posner (1996, p. 39), for example, points out that "the local trial bar is invariably the major source of campaign contributions to judicial candidates." At a given moment, some trial lawyers are working for the plaintiff and others for the defense. Nevertheless, in general, all trial lawyers are interested in larger awards. Larger awards mean larger fees, whether one works for the plaintiff or for the defense. Consider two judges who rule in the plaintiff's favor equally often, but one of whom tends to be more generous in the granting of awards. Defense and plaintiffs' lawyers will both prefer that the more generous judge be elected because generous judges increase the demand for both plaintiff and defense lawyers. Judges who grant large awards will find fundraising for their campaigns easier than their more "stingy" colleagues. Thus, even if every judge applies the law with no consideration whatsoever for political factors, we can expect that over time generous judges will be selected in states with an elected judiciary.

The campaign-contribution theory implies that awards in general should be higher in partisan-elected states. To reach the conclusion that awards against out-of-state defendants will be especially high, we need the supplementary hypothesis that local defendants (voters) will discipline judges who raise in-state awards. In-state defendants may be able to counter the campaign contributions of trial lawyers through their votes, but no such counter is available to out-of-state defendants. Thus, the elasticity of awards against out-of-state defendants (with respect to lawyer campaign contributions) is larger than is the elasticity of awards against local defendants.

A third explanation for why awards in cases with out-of-state defendants are larger in partisan-elected states than in other states is that partisan elections bring more extreme judges to the bench. "Extreme" in this context means having a tendency to give either significantly higher-than-average or significantly lower-than-average awards. Since awards are bounded below by zero, however, a greater variance in award decisions implies a larger mean award. Like the campaign-contribution theory, the variance theory implies that awards in general will be higher in partisan-elected states. With the supplementary hypothesis that local defendants can discipline judges who grant large awards against local defendants, the theory also implies that awards against out-of-state defendants will be especially high. The variance theory differs from the plaintiff-voter and campaign-contribution theories in that the increase in awards is not a direct consequence of partisan elections but a byproduct of higher judicial variance. As noted above, researchers have not found any significant differences in judicial characteristics across electoral systems, but easily observable characteristics do not exhaust the many margins on which judges may differ. Moreover, mean judicial characteristics may be similar across systems, yet partisan elections still cause large differences in awards if those differences are due to a handful of judges.

Each of these theories focuses on judicial incentives or characteristics. Judges, however, directly decide only a minority of tort cases, perhaps as few as 10 percent overall (the rate varies with the type of case). Nevertheless, judges have significant control over the trial outcome. Judges must interpret the law for juries, instruct the juries, allow or disallow objections, rule on motions and counter-motions, limit or not limit the lawyers to certain theories of liability and damages, etc. Our thesis does not require that partisan-elected judges make blatantly biased rulings. All the thesis requires is that compared to other judges, partisan-elected judges make marginal changes in rulings that tend in the direction of supporting larger awards.

Since almost all personal-injury cases are tried by jury, we cannot absolutely rule out the hypothesis that juries in states that elect their judges using partisan elections are especially likely to grant large awards against out-of-state defendants. Nevertheless, three pieces of evidence, plus Occam's razor, suggest that the explanation for our results lies in judges, not juries. First, the limited evidence (see below) from judge trials is consistent with the jury evidence. Second, we control for the most obvious characteristic that might affect jury awards: poverty rates of the jury pool. Although we find that local poverty does increase awards (the "Bronx effect"), it is not responsible for the partisan-electoral effect. Third, if juries were responsible for our results, we would also expect to see larger awards against out-of-state defendants in partisan-elected states in cases presided over by federal judges (most tort trials are jury trials in both federal and state courts). We show below, however, that when federal judges are presiding, awards against out-of-state defendants are not significantly larger in partisan-elected states as compared to non-partisan states.

EXPLORATORY DATA ANALYSIS:
PARTISAN VS. NON-PARTISAN STATE COURT CASES

The data on torts is similar to that described in Chapter 2 and was extracted from Jury Verdict Research's *Personal Injury Verdicts and Settlements* on CD-ROM. Table 1 presents means for the total award and the win rate broken down by various categories of case. The breakdown is similar to that found in other data sets.

The data set contains the name of the defendant, which may be either a business or an individual, but it does not give an address for the defendant. Nor do we have addresses for the plaintiffs, all of whom are individuals. We were able to assign an in-state or an out-of-state classification for each business defendant in our sample by using the COMP database to locate the headquarters of each business. The COMP database contains information on more than 140,000 private and public companies. We were able to locate the headquarters of a majority of the companies in our sample. We assumed that any company that we could not find in the database (e.g., Alex's Muffler Shop) was headquartered locally, that is to say, in the state in which the trial occurred. We were not able to locate the residences of the individual plaintiffs or defendants in our sample and, by default, assume that each individual resides in the state in which

TABLE 1 Expected Awards and Win Rates by Trial Category.

	Expected Total Award	Win Rate	Trials
All	$332,285	0.556	52,551
Product Liability	$1,457,984	.427	2,134
Medical Malpractice	$598,096	.328	6,147
Auto	$159,734	.656	24,856
Premises Liability	$162,975	.45	7,916

the trial occurs. Although it is possible to sue in a state other than the one in which you reside, it is troublesome and thus rare.[8]

In Table 2, we perform a simple difference in means test by regressing the total award on a constant and four dummy variables: Partisan Out, Partisan In, NonPartisan Out, and NonPartisan In. Partisan Out denotes trials in partisan states with out-of-state business defendants; the other variables are defined similarly. The coefficient on the constant term is the average award in non-business cases. The coefficients on the other variables are the differences between cases of that type and the average non-business case.

In partisan states, the average award against an out-of-state business defendant is $936,190, which is $527,740 larger than the average award against an in-state business defendant ($936,190–$408,450). In nonpartisan states, the average award against an out-of-state business defendant is only $272,780, which is only $138,730 larger than the average award against an in-state business. The difference between the differences (Partisan Out–NonPartisan Out) measures the total "partisan effect." Awards against out-of-state businesses are $663,410 higher in partisan than in nonpartisan states. The difference is statistically significant at the (far) greater than 1 percent level, ($F_{[1,52540]}=16.31$ with $p=0.0001$). This evidence supports the hypothesis that awards against out-of-state businesses are significantly higher in states with partisan elections than in states that use other selection mechanisms.

The total partisan effect, Partisan Out–NonPartisan Out, com-

TABLE 2 Difference in Means, Medians, 75th Percentiles, Judge Only.

Variable	Total Award (all awards)	Medians (pos. awards)	75th Percentile (pos. awards)	Judge Cases Only
Constant (Non-Business Cases)	$252,540*** (19,524)	$34,000 [20,033]	$164,194 [20,033]	$204,838*** (25,914)
Partisan Out	$936,190*** (143,800)	$116,942 [320]	$800,000 [320]	$319,908* (178,696)
Partisan In	$408,450*** (60,090)	$102,505 [2,256]	$526,668 [2,256]	$16,801 (81,869)
NonPartisan Out	$272,780*** (84,070)	$79,577 [1,261]	$341,638 [1,261]	$115,143 (132,549)
NonPartisan In	$138,730*** (43,003)	$88,572 [5,423]	$367,708 [5,423]	$15,529 (70,453)
Number of Cases	53,545	53,545	53,545	3,712

Differences in Differences

	Total Award (all awards)	Medians (pos. awards)	75th Percentile (pos. awards)	Judge Cases Only
Partisan Out NonPartisan Out	936,190– 272,780= 527,740*** p=0.0001	116,942– 79,577= 37365*** p=0.0084[nb]	800,000– 526,668= 458,362*** p=0.0000[nb]	319,908– 115,143= 204,765 p=0.5

[nb]The p-values in the median and 75th percentile columns were calculated using the bootstrap method.

***Significant at the .01 level

Note: In the total awards regression awards are expressed as differences from the average non-business award (constant). In the median and 75th percentile columns, the awards are expressed as exact values, not as differences from non-business cases.

OLS standard errors are in parentheses in the total award column. Number of observations in each category are indicated in brackets in the other columns.

bines a partisan out-of-state effect with a partisan business effect. Awards against out-of-state comapanies in partisan-elected states may be higher than similar cases in nonpartisan states because awards are higher against out-of-state companies in partisan states (the partisan out-of-state effect) or because awards against businesses in general are higher in partisan states (the partisan business effect). The two effects can be decomposed. The partisan out-of-state effect is measured by (Partisan Out–Partisan In)–(NonPartisan Out–NonPartisan In). By subtracting out awards against in-state businesses, we control for any increase in awards against businesses in general in partisan-elected states, thus isolating the partisan out-of-state effect. The partisan out-of-state effect has value \$393,690(F[1,52540]=4.84 and p=0.027). The partisan-business effect is measured by (Partisan In–NonPartisan In) and has a value of \$269,720(F[1,52540]=15.7801, p=.0001). Awards against businesses in general are larger in partisan states than in non-partisan states, but the majority of the partisan effect is due to a bias against *out-of-state* business defendants.

Trial awards are highly right-skewed and most of the partisan-electoral effect comes from an increase in the right-hand tail of the distribution of awards. Columns 2 and 3 of Table 2 present the median award and the award at the 75th percentile in all the case types. Median awards in cases with out-of-state defendants are \$37,365 larger in partisan-elected states than in nonpartisan states. The difference is statistically significant at the greater than 1 percent level. As the percentile increases, the difference in awards between partisan states and nonpartisan states increases. At the 75th percentile, awards against out-of-state defendants are \$458,362 larger in partisan-elected states than in other states.

Column 4 of Table 2 presents results looking only at judge-decided trials. The judge and jury samples are not directly comparable since the sample of cases going to trial before a judge are quite different from those going to trial before a jury (see Chapter 3). In particular, judges deal with the types of cases likely to generate low awards (e.g., premises liability and auto cases) in much greater proportion than do juries. As a result, the mean award in judge trials is well below the mean jury award. Judge trials are also quite rare in personal-injury lawsuits as more than 90 percent of these trials are tried before juries. We should not expect, therefore, that the judge and jury results will be similar. Nevertheless, when the defendant is out-of-state the mean award in partisan states is over \$200,000 higher than the mean award in non-partisan states. The difference between the two awards, however, is not statistically significant at conventional levels probably because the sample size is so small (there are only 60 out-of-state defendants in partisan states and only 111 out-of-state defendants in nonpartisan states). In the remainder of the chapter, we take advantage of our large data set by focusing on the combined judge and jury sample (results do not change in a jury-only sample).

Although suggestive, these differences in means and medians raise the question of whether the larger awards in partisan states are caused by differences in the electoral system or by some other differences which are merely correlated with differences in the electoral system. In the following section, we refine the difference-in-differences analysis to control for a variety of other potential influences. In particular, to properly account for selection effects, we model the process that transforms a dispute into a trial into a winning case.

ESTIMATION PROCEDURE: OVERVIEW

In this section, we control for many other variables that could affect awards. Our data set has descriptive information on the victim's injury. We code this information into nine exclusive and exhaustive variables: LLIFE, Major Injury, Minor Injury, Emotional Distress, Rape, Sexual Assault, Sexual Harassment, Bad Faith, and Wrongful Termination. LLIFE is the expected years of life left in a case involving a death. The remaining injury variables are dummy variables. If the victim suffered a permanent injury such as loss of limb, brain damage, or blindness, Major is set equal to one. Minor injuries are those that are (potentially) temporary, including, for example, broken arms, broken legs, concussions, or wounds. Emotional Distress indicates cases in which the victim suffered emotional or psychological injuries. Rape, Sexual Assault and Sexual Harassment are self-explanatory. Bad Faith cases are those in which a plaintiff sues an insurance company for denying a claim. The injury in bad-faith cases is the denial of the claim, not a physical injury. In a Wrongful Termination case, the plaintiff sues his ex-employer for wrongful dismissal. Together these variables control for the severity of the plaintiff's injury. To prevent perfect co-linearity with the intercept term, we suppress Wrongful Termination. As in earlier regressions, we include case type variables.

We also include a number of legal variables that may affect liability. A dummy variable, Weak Joint and Several, is set equal to one if the state has created significant exceptions to the joint and several liability rule (many states have eliminated the rule in product liability cases and weakened it in other types of cases) and there is more than one defendant. The NonEconomic Cap is set equal to one if state law puts a cap on damages due to pain and suffering or other noneconomic losses. Under the collateral sources rule, payments to the plaintiff from a third party (i.e., insurance company) are not deducted from damages due from the defendant. If Collateral Sources is set equal to one, the collateral sources rule is weakened so that some offset is allowed. In states with an Evidence Standard, the defendant's behavior must "clearly and convincingly" be shown to have exhibited "reckless disregard" or "malice" for punitive damages to be awarded. In states with bifurcated trials, punitive damages claims may be considered separately from compensatory claims. Since a bifurcated trial usually only occurs at the request of the defendant, we expect that bifurcated trials will reduce awards. No Punitive is a dummy variable set equal to one if the state "prohibits" punitive damages.[9] Punitive Cap is set equal to one if the state in which the trial occurs caps punitive damages either absolutely or relative to compensatory damages (for example, punitive damages cannot exceed compensatory damages by more than three times). We expect that weakening the joint and several rule will decrease awards and thus have a negative sign, while NonEconomic Cap, Collateral Source, Evidence Standard, Bifurcated Trial, No Punitive and Punitive Cap variables will all reduce compensatory or punitive damages and thus have negative signs. As before, we include the local poverty rate.

The test variables Partisan Out, Partisan In, NonPartisan Out, and NonPartisan In are as described above.

Also, to observe an award, the case must have failed to settle and the plaintiff must have won the case. To account for the selection effect, we estimate the award at trial using what is known as the Heckman procedure. Readers who are interested in the details and results from the other equations of the model can consult Helland and Tabarrok (2002). In this chapter, we focus on the partisan electoral hypothesis.

RESULTS FROM THE AWARD EQUATION

Our discussion of the results will focus on a few illustrative variables rather than pedantically mentioning each in turn. The dependent variable is the natural log of the total award. All non-dummy variables are also in natural logs. Results can be found in Table 3.

The injury variables are significant and of the expected sign. For comparison purposes, the mean dollar award conditional on winning is $599,000 while the median dollar award is $48,604 (the exponential of the mean log award is close to the median dollar award). If the victim died with an expected 40 years of life remaining (i.e., at an approximate age of 35 years old) the mean dollar award increases to $2.92 million and the median dollar award increases to $237,200. Alternatively expressed, if the victim dies at approximately age 35, the award increases by 437 percent.[10] A major injury increases awards by 179 percent[11] and a minor injury decreases awards by 50 percent. Awards are approximately double (103 percent higher) in product liability cases than in otherwise similar cases. A closely related puzzle is that awards in auto cases are about half the size of awards in otherwise similar cases. Thus, a plaintiff is rewarded much more highly if he loses his arm in a lawnmower accident (product liability) than if he loses an arm in an automobile accident. These results suggest a "deep pockets" effect, although other explanations are possible. Awards could be higher in product liability cases; for example, because these cases are more difficult to detect than auto accidents.

TABLE 3 State Regression Results.

Variable	Equation — Trial Award
Constant	13.128*** (1.3084)
Expected Years of Life Left	0.45591*** (.02967)
Major Injury	1.0286*** (.091558)
Minor Injury	−0.69608*** (.085231)
Emotional Distress	−1.0132*** (0.095743)
Rape	1.5684*** (.27086)
Sexual Assault	1.2839*** (.16177)
Sexual Harassment	−0.26084 (.39584)
Bad Faith	−.18688 (.13875)
Product Liability	0.71113* (.38531)
Medical Malpractice	0.73897 (.71503)
Auto	−0.66701** (.28065)
Premises Liability	−.16022 (.30666)
Weak Joint and Several Liability	0.006289 (0.054663)
NonEconomic Cap	−0.38883*** (0.04349)
Collateral Sources	0.36266*** (.022871)
No Punitive	0.14863 (0.14293)

*Significant at the greater than 0.1 level.
**Significant at the greater than .05 level.
***Significant at the greater than .01 level.
Note: OLS equations show corrected standard errors in parentheses (see text). Marginal effects are computed at the means.

TABLE 3 State Regression Results. (*cont.*)

Punitive Cap	−0.32897*** (.022675)
Evidence Standard	0.24964*** (.02590)
Bifurcated Trial	−0.071488 (.48386)
Poverty	0.94045*** (.19452)
Partisan Out	0.70742*** (.10477)
Partisan In	0.47967*** (.045607)
NonPartisan Out	.35693*** (.05665)
NonPartisan In	.35481*** (.0338)
IMR Settle	−1.2063*** (.053352)
IMR Win	−0.082936 (1.8428)
Number of Cases	29,238

Not surprisingly, given the results of Chapter 2, the greater the local poverty rate, the higher the award, holding all else equal. The poverty variable is highly statistically significant ($p=0.00001$) and also economically meaningful.

The legal variables are not all significant or of the expected sign. Weakening the joint and several rule appears to have no effect on awards. Caps on damages due to pain and suffering reduce awards on average by 32 percent. We expected the Collateral Sources and the Evidence Standard to have negative signs, but they are both statistically significant with positive signs; they raise awards by 36 percent and 24 percent, respectively. States with larger awards may be more likely to weaken the collateral-sources rule and enact evidence standards. Endogeneity problems may thus prevent accurate estimation of the effect of these variables in a cross-section regression. (Since we include the legal variables only to control for factors, other than electoral systems, that cause differences in awards across the states, the difficulty in interpretation is not material to our primary results.) As expected, caps on punitive damages reduce awards (by 28 percent) as do bifurcated trials (-6.8 percent).

Our primary hypothesis concerns the electoral variables: Partisan Out, Partisan In, NonPartisan Out, and NonPartisan In. Awards against out-of-state businesses are 42 percent larger in partisan states than in nonpartisan states. Put differently, moving an otherwise average case with an out-of-state defendant from a nonpartisan to a partisan state raises the expected award by $362,988. The partisan effect is statistically significant at the greater than 1 percent level.[12] It is worth emphasizing that the $362,967 partisan-election effect exists after controlling for a wide variety of potential differences in cases across the states, including differences in injuries, state incomes, and major laws. The coefficients on NonPartisan Out and on NonPartisan In are almost identical, which suggests that there is little or no penalty against out-of-state businesses in nonpartisan states. In contrast, the coefficient on Partisan Out is larger than that on Partisan In, and both coefficients are larger than their nonpartisan state counterparts. The evidence, therefore, suggests that in partisan-elected states awards against businesses are higher than in other states and awards against out-of-state businesses are especially high.[13]

As noted earlier, we can break the partisan effect into partisan out-of-state and partisan-business effects. The partisan out-of-state effect is measured by (Partisan Out–Partisan In)–(NonPartisan Out–NonPartisan In). The partisan out-of-state effect accounts for $230,092 of the $362,988 total partisan effect. The remaining $132,897 is accounted for by the partisan-business effect. As we found in the simple difference of means estimates, awards are higher in partisan - elected states, both because awards against businesses are higher and because awards against out-of-state businesses are especially high.[14]

In Table 4, we test the robustness of the partisan-electoral effect.

In Column 1, we run the same regression as earlier, but without any selection effects (for clarity we present only the electoral variables). We find that awards against out-of-state businesses are 31 percent larger in partisan states than in nonpartisan states. The difference is statistically significant at the just over 1 percent level. Since the partisan-electoral effect is robust to the exclusion of selection effects, none of the details of our estimation technique, such as our creation of the expected award variables, are driving our results.

As a second robustness test, we add state-specific fixed-effects to the win and award equations. (For an explanation of state fixed effects see chapter 2. Briefly, we allow each state to have its own mean award and win rate thereby removing a source of bias from our estimation.).

TABLE 4 Robustness Tests.

Variables	No Selection Effects	State Fixed Effects[b]	Business Cases Only	Prod/Med Only
Partisan Out	.679449*** (.104679)	.70156*** (.10250)	.429695*** (.108813)	.9075*** (.2800)
Partisan In	.464236*** (.04318)	.33804*** (.045359)	.210822*** (.051442)	−.1203 (.1283)
NonPartisan Out	.409429*** (.0549311)	.43537*** (.053965)	02011229 (.0587857)	.1928 (.1572)
NonPartisan In[a]	.412717*** (.030204)	.43185*** (.030457)	.	.1576 (.1015)
Number of Cases	29,238	29,238	9,245	2,929

Differences in Differences

Partisan Out NonPartisan Out	$(e^{.0.679-.409}-1)=$ .309*** p=0.0191	$(e^{.701-.435}-1)=$ .304** p=0.0189	$(e^{.429-.02}-1)=$ .50*** p=0.000419	$(e^{.907-.192}-1)=1.0$** p=0.0160

* Significant at greater than 0.1 level.

** Significant at greater than 0.05 level.

** Significant at greater than 0.01 level.

OLS corrected standard errors in parentheses.

[a]NonPartisan In was suppressed in the business cases only regression to prevent perfect co-linearity with the intercept.

[b]OLS standard errors were used in this regression (see text).

Award and win rates appear to vary somewhat across the states, but the variation is not correlated to the electoral variables. In this regression, we estimate that awards against out-of-state businesses are 30 percent greater in partisan states than in nonpartisan states. The difference is statistically significant at the just over 1 percent level.[15]

The reference case in our earlier regressions was a nonbusiness case. The partisan-electoral effect is estimated on the basis of cases with business defendants because only in these cases can we easily identify in-state and out-of-state defendants. We include nonbusiness cases in our regressions because we are interested in the coefficients of nonelectoral variables such as poverty and because the inclusion of nonbusiness cases improves the estimates of the nonelectoral variables. Better estimates of the nonelectoral variables in turn allow for better estimation of the electoral variables. In Column 3 of Table 4, we estimate the model using business cases only to show that this restriction is not driving our results. Using business cases only, we find that awards in partisan states with out-of-state defendants are 50 percent larger than awards against out-of-state defendants in nonpartisan states. The difference is statistically significant at the greater than 1 percent level.

Our fourth robustness test restricts the sample to cases of special interest, product liability, and medical malpractice cases. Again, we find that awards against out-of-state defendants are much higher in partisan states than in nonpartisan states. The difference is statistically significant at the greater than 5 percent level.

DIVERSITY-OF-CITIZENSHIP CASES

The U.S. Constitution (Article III, Section 2(1)) gives the federal courts the power to decide controversies between citizens of different states. Historically, federal diversity jurisdiction was supported by out-of-state businesses that feared they would be disadvantaged in pro-plaintiff/pro-debtor state courts (Friendly 1928). Today lawyers continue to cite out-of-state and anti-business bias as one reason for removing cases to federal court (Miller 1992). For more than a century, federal judges decided diversity-of-citizenship cases based on federal common law. The Supreme Court, however, overturned this rule in the 1938 case *Erie Railroad v. Tompkins* (304 U.S. p. 64). Since the 1938 Supreme Court decision, diversity-of-citizenship cases have been decided on the basis of state law.[16]

Even when federal judges apply state law, comparing federal and state cases is problematic because of multiple sample-selection problems. Cases that go to federal court are not a random selection of state cases. Clearly, diversity-of-citizenship cases require that the plaintiff be suing a citizen of another state. In addition, in order to bring a diversity-of-citizenship case to federal court, the plaintiff must claim damages of at least $50,000 (since raised to $75,000). Other differences in the sample of cases going to federal court may be unobserved. Furthermore, we have to be careful to allow settlement behavior to differ in the two samples. Posner (1996) suggests, for example, that federal courts are more predictable than state courts. If the variance of the outcome is lower in federal court then, ceterius paribus, the probability of settling should be higher and, thus, a different sample of cases go to trial in federal courts than in state courts.

Our strategy for controlling for these issues is twofold. Most importantly, we do not directly compare state cases to federal cases. Instead, we follow our earlier differences-in-differences method. We compare awards in cases where federal judges apply the law of partisan-elected states with awards in cases where federal judges apply the law of nonpartisan states. This gives us the Federal Difference (Partisan–NonPartisan)$_{Fed}$. Using a similar sample of cases (cases involving out of-state businesses), we create the State Difference (Partisan–NonPartisan)$_{State}$. If all of the partisan election effect is due to differences in the law of torts in partisan-elected states, then the Federal and State difference should be equal, that is to say, (Partisan–Non-

Partisan)$_{Fed}$–(Partisan–NonPartisan)$_{State}$=0. If the partisan-election effect is due to partisan-elected judges interpreting essentially the same law differently than judges in other states, then the State Difference should be much larger than the Federal Difference. The advantage of the differences-in-differences method is that it measures exclusively the partisan-election effect, thus controlling for any other differences in federal and state cases.

The second part of our strategy for controlling sample-selection problems uses the Heckman (1979) two-step method. Essentially we add another level of selection, the forum choice, to our earlier model. The sample of cases is all cases involving out-of-state businesses. Each of these cases could potentially go to either federal or state court. Again, see Helland and Tabarrok (2002) for more details on the econometric procedure and results.

RESULTS

We are primarily interested in the award equations and, in particular, we wish to compare (Partisan–NonPartisan)$_{State}$ and (Partisan–NonPartisan)$_{Fed}$.[17] We define Partisan as a dummy variable equal to one if the case in question took place in a state with partisan elected judges.[18] (Partisan–NonPartisan)$_{State}$ is thus equal to the coefficient on Partisan in the state regression and (Partisan–NonPartisan)$_{Fed}$ is equal to the coefficient on Partisan in the federal regression. Results on the award regression are presented in Table 5. Most importantly, Partisan has a coefficient of .20568 (statistically significant at the 10 percent level) in the state regression, but a nonstatistically significant coefficient of .12339 in the federal regression. Awards are thus larger in partisan-elected states when state judges are deciding cases, but not when nonelected federal judges with life tenure are deciding cases. Moving an otherwise average case from a nonpartisan state to a partisan state in the state courts raises the expected award by

TABLE 5 Diversity Jurisdiction Regressions.

Variable	Equation	
	State Trial Award (SA)	Federal Trial Award (FA)
Constant	23.468 (22.065)	9.7548* (5.2284)
Expected Years of Life Left (LLife)	0.73887 (.59406))	0.35046** (0.17548)
Major Injury	0.77818*** (.294)	0.69981** (0.27889)
Minor Injury	−0.27835* (.27671)	0.052187 (0.33046)
Emotional Distress	−.056708 (.47335	−.83598 (.96127)
Bad Faith	−0.51513 (.31419)	0.082754 (0.32952)
Product Liability	7.9794 (9.9903)	.031906 (1.1737)
Medical Malpractice	11.105 (14.793)	.29501 (1.83)
Auto	−3.9189 (7.5580)	−2.5172 (2.1438)
Premises Liability	−0.59280 (.38107)	−1.6337** (0.67213)
Weak Joint and Several Liability	0.0949 (.29431)	0.23572 (.21536)
Non-Economic Cap	−0.18340* (.11036)	0.084092 (.16731)
Collateral Sources	.38053*** (.074358)	0.085827 (.13338)
No Punitive	.11385 (2.4729)	.31302 (.56295)
Punitive Cap	−0.26556*** (.10113)	−.21347 (.23972)
Evidence Standard	0.42125*** (.10398)	.14723 (.18421)
Number of Defendants	.96580*** (.18248)	
Poverty	1.4331* (.78213)	0.91642 (1.6908)

TABLE 5 Diversity Jurisdiction Regressions. (*cont.*)

Variable	Equation	
	State Trial Award (SA)	Federal Trial Award (FA)
Partisan	0.20568* (.12411)	.12339 (.15279)
IMR FC	4.1657*** (1.1981)	2.047 (1.977)
IMR T	−0.7701*** (.26566)	1.4230 (1.4518)
IMR W	−21.617 (33.099)	−1.0549 (6.0838)
Number of Cases	2,120	1,138

23 percent, or $233,157, evaluated at the mean of the federal sample. Moving a case from a nonpartisan state to a partisan state in the federal courts, however, does not systematically increase the award.

In Table 6, we perform two robustness tests. The diversity jurisdiction regressions have much smaller sample sizes than our earlier cross-state regression. Some of the regression coefficients in the diversity regressions are clearly not good estimates of the population parameters. The coefficient on Medical Malpractice in the state diversity regression (SA), for example, is 11, much larger than in the state regressions and far larger than is reasonable. The estimate is, of course, appropriate for the sample, but there are only seventeen medical malpractice trials in the state diversity regression, and it so happens that these few trials resulted in large awards that are not representative of the population. We are almost entirely interested in the coefficient on Partisan, however, so imprecision in the estimation of control variables is not necessarily disturbing. To improve efficiency, however, we performed the following analysis: We restricted the beta coefficients in the diversity jurisdiction equation to have the same values as is in the earlier state regression, with the exception of the endogenous sample selection parameters, a constant, and Partisan, which were left unrestricted. If the beta coefficients from the

TABLE 6 Robustness Test.

	With Restricted Nonelectoral Coefficients	With Circuit/ Regional Dummies Coefficient on Partisan
State Trial Award	0.24708[**] (0.10043)	0.43398[**] (0.14127)
Federal Trial Award	0.13941 (0.10416)	0.16609 (0.19766)

*Significant at the 0.1 level.
**Significant at the .05 level.
**Significant at the .01 level.
Note: OLS equations show corrected standard errors in parentheses (see text).

state regression, which are well-estimated because of the large sample size, are better estimates of the true betas than are the unrestricted betas from the small sample diversity-jurisdiction equation, then imposing these restrictions will improve the efficiency of estimation of the unrestricted parameters. Results on Partisan from the restricted regression are also presented in Column 1 of Table 6. Partisan has a statistically significant (at the 5 percent level) coefficient of .24708 in the state regression and a statistically insignificant coefficient of .13941 in the federal regression. Thus, improving the efficiency of the estimates strengthens the conclusion that awards are larger in states with partisan-elected judges when state judges make decisions, but not when federal judges make decisions using the same set of laws. The estimates from the unrestricted and restricted state diversity-of-citizenship equations suggest that awards are 21 percent to 28 percent higher in partisan states with out-of-state defendants than in other states. Evaluated at the mean of the state diversity-of-citizenship sample, awards are higher by between $233,157 and $286,169.

Observers of the judicial process have long argued that federal circuit courts differ in their interpretations of the law (for a review see Rowland and Carp 1996). We add circuit dummies to the award and win equations to control for any systematic differences in awards across federal circuits. Since circuits often overlap with regions, we also include the same set of dummies in the state regression. When we control for circuit/regional effects, we find that the coefficient on Partisan in the federal regression is virtually unchanged. It remains small and statistically insignificant. The coefficient on Partisan in the state regression, however, increases in size and statistical significance. The coefficient suggests that awards against out-of-state businesses may be as much as 54 percent larger in partisan states than in nonpartisan states. Thus, we continue to find that awards in cases with out-of-state defendants are larger in partisan-elected states when state judges are deciding cases but not when nonelected federal judges with life tenure are deciding cases.

CONCLUSIONS

Judges respond to incentives just like other politicians. Understanding judicial behavior, therefore, requires an understanding of incentive structures. In ten states, judges are elected on competitive partisan ballots. Partisan-elected judges must cater to their constituents, and they must raise campaign funds in order to get elected. The variance of judicial award decisions may also be larger in partisan-elected states (causing an increase in mean awards since awards are bounded below by zero). We hypothesized that these forces would increase awards in partisan-elected states relative to other states, particularly awards against out-of-state businesses. The evidence, both from the cross-state regressions and from diversity-of-citizenship cases, strongly supports the partisan-election hypothesis. In cases involving out-of-state defendants and in-state plaintiffs, the average award (conditional upon winning) is \$362,988 higher in partisan states than in nonpartisan states; \$230,092 of the larger award is due to a bias against out-of-state defendants, and the remainder is due to generally higher awards against businesses in partisan states.

Awards might be higher in partisan-elected states because of differences in the law in those states or because of differences in the judicial incentive structure. (Of course, these possibilities are not exclusive; differences in the law could be caused by differences in the incentive structure.) To test these alternative possibilities, we compared awards in cases decided by unelected, lifetime-tenured federal judges with awards in cases decided by state judges, when both apply state law. More precisely, we compared the difference in awards in partisan and nonpartisan states in cases decided by federal judges with the difference in awards in partisan states and nonpartisan states when cases were decided by state judges. We found that awards were higher in partisan-elected states only when the cases were decided by state judges. Our evidence suggests that the primary reason awards are higher in partisan-elected states is not because of differences in law across the states but rather because partisan-elected judges decide cases differently than judges selected in other ways.

5

Two Cheers for Contingent Fees

INTRODUCTION

Tort awards have increased dramatically in recent decades (Helland, Klick, and Tabarrok 2005). Firms avoid producing risky yet useful devices like vaccines and small airplanes, and local communities sometimes no longer provide swimming pools and playgrounds for fear of lawsuits. Product liability awards and the threat of lawsuits pushed many companies into bankruptcy, despite increases in safety (Priest 1991). Increases in the number of medical malpractice cases and the height of awards pushed insurance premiums higher and doctors began to exit from hard-hit specialties like obstetrics.[1] Some consumers who had never sued anyone in their life suddenly and unwittingly found themselves a party to half a dozen cases a year as class-action suits multiplied in frequency (Hensler 2001).

If America has been called "Lawsuit Hell," contingent-fee lawyers have often been cast as the devils. In the midst of increased filings and escalating awards, it was difficult not to notice that some plaintiffs' lawyers were becoming very rich. In some cases (prominently, the state cases against tobacco firms), trial lawyers collected several billion dollars.[2] The astronomical fees earned by some trial lawyers have become the stuff of front-page newspaper coverage and of a best-selling novel (Langley 2004 and Grisham 2003). The profits earned by an increasingly resourceful, organized and aggressive "litigation industry," and especially the plow-back of those profits into the political system and into ever-more creative litigation campaigns, has caused considerable alarm not only—and predictably—among corporate executives, but also among journalists and other observers who hold no particular brief for corporate defendants (Schroeder 2001; Thomas and Garber 2004; Hollandsworth 1996).

The trial lawyers' riches per se provide no cause for concern. Americans have a very high tolerance for fabulous wealth. Bill Gates and Warren Buffett are objects of admiration, not envy. However, unlike computer and software production, equity investing, or for that matter movie entertainment (where superstars also earn exorbitant returns), liability litigation is not a productive enterprise. Its central purpose is the redistribution rather than the creation of wealth—sometimes for good but, by all indications, often for ill. The lawyers' fees, both on the defense and on the plaintiff's side, are a pure transaction cost. And as those transaction costs have mounted, a natural suspicion has arisen that the trial bar's fee arrangements may be a driving force behind the liability explosion. Contingent fees and the lawyers who accept them have been denounced as unwarranted, unethical, and uncivilized (Brickman 2003, 653–660; Olson 1991). Several prominent observers have argued that contingent fees encourage excessive and frivolous litigation and, moreover, create conflicts of interest between client and attorney, especially with respect to settlement decisions (MacKinnon 1964; Miller 1987; Bernstein 1996; Olson 1991).

These observations and contentions have prompted tort reformers to demand, in addition to substantive legal reforms (such as caps on nonmonetary damages) caps or limitations on contingent fees. A number of states enacted contingent-fee limitations as early as the 1970s and throughout the 1980s (see Table 1). Reform activity on this front continued in tandem with the continued proliferation of high-dollar verdicts. For example, the U.S. Congress has considered the imposition of a federal excise tax on "excessive" attorneys fees, especially the fees collected in connection with the states' anti-tobacco litigation.[3] Most recently, in November 2004, the Florida voters approved a self-executing amendment to the state's constitution which caps attorney fees at 30 percent of the first $250,000 in damages awarded and at 10 percent for any award amount above that level.

As we have discussed, we have considerable sympathy with the general case for tort reform. For reasons explained in this chapter, however, we question the merits of contingent-fee limitations. Those measures have been enacted without any empirical evidence that contingent fees were either responsible for the liability crisis or that limiting them would produce benefits. Based on the evidence presented here, we are persuaded that restrictions on contingent fees are for the most part unjustified and, moreover, produce unintended negative consequences. Most likely, contingent-fee caps or limitations, which operate as a tax on the lawyer's compensation, will tend to wash *more* low-value "junk suits" into the legal system.

It is important to note the limitations of this argument. Overwhelmingly, the anecdotal empirical ammunition against contingent fees comes from class-action lawsuits or from mass-tort litigation, such as asbestos litigation. Exorbitant attorneys' fee awards in consumer class-action suits that yield nothing but valueless coupons for the purported plaintiff class have drawn sharp criticism from legal scholars and consumer activists,[4] and they have produced interventions by the Federal Trade Commission's Consumer Protection office and, most recently, federal legislative reform.[5] Similarly, the near-criminal practices attendant to the mass production of asbestos, fen phen, and similar claims have prompted justifiably harsh criticism and, at long last, probing judicial scrutiny (Brickman 2004; Frankel 2005, 92).

Both the extensive literature and the targeted federal interventions, however, illustrate that class-action suits are a special problem, both as an empirical matter and in terms of their underlying economics. We put those problems aside for one excellent reason:

The state contingent-fee limitations here at issue do not apply to class actions or mass torts only. In point of fact, many of these state-imposed limitations are targeted at contingent fees in medical-malpractice cases, where those forms of actions are exceptionally rare. It is in those traditional, individual suits over medical malpractice and personal injury that contingent-fee limitations, rather than contingent fees themselves, are likely to produce adverse consequences.

We begin by discussing the basic economic theory of contingent fees, which provides potent reasons to believe that such arrangements may be efficient. Based on that discussion, we present empirical evidence—discussed in a more extensive and more technical version in an earlier article of ours (Helland and Tabarrok 2003)—showing that contingent-fee limitations tend to increase the frequency of low-value claims. We then discuss, in light of theoretical considerations and empirical evidence, the most common arguments against contingent fees: the possibility of asymmetrical incentives that may induce lawyers to act at variance with their clients' best interests; the charge that contingent fees may generate excess returns (or "rents") for lawyers; and the contention that contingent-fees may be good for the clients (and for that matter, the lawyers), but harmful to society as a whole. We conclude that contingent-fee caps are a poor proxy for better-targeted reforms that would address the true problems of the liability system.

CONTINGENT FEES: ECONOMIC FUNDAMENTALS

We are, as noted, critical of modern tort litigation—and yet cautiously supportive of the contingent-fee arrangements that seem to play such a big role in that industry. Is this not a mild case of schizophrenia?

The short answer is, no. Contingent-fee arrangements are *contracts*, and along with the vast majority of economists, we start with the presumption that self-interest pushes private bargains toward efficiency. The crucial problem in tort law is that there is not enough contract.[6] Restrictions on contingent fees are restrictions on the freedom to contract and, as such, must pass a high hurdle to be justified. The presumption for contracts is rebuttable. But in examining well-accepted contractual practices, one ought to start with the premise of contractual efficiency, even when neither the theorists, nor for that matter market participants themselves, can conclusively explain *why* the arrangements are efficient (Easterbrook 1984, 1, 9–10).

Contingent fees *are* a widespread practice. They have been common in the United States for at least one hundred years, long before onset of the liability crisis.[7] Reasons that help explain the practice are not hard to come by.

Reducing monitoring costs. Some benefits of contingent fees are well-agreed upon. It is difficult for a plaintiff to evaluate how much effort a lawyer puts into a case. Time-sheets are not easily verifiable and, even if they were, hours are not the same as effort. If the plaintiff loses his case, did he lose because his lawyer was ill-prepared? Or was it because the case lacked merit? If the plaintiff wins, would the award amount have been greater with more effort? A plaintiff who cannot answers these questions will look for some contractual device that induces attorney effort without requiring that the plaintiff be well-informed.

There are several ways of accomplishing that objective. One device is a "conditional fee"—that is, a bonus tied to winning, but not to the amount of the award. Thus, an arrangement providing for fees of $1,000 in the event of a loss and $2,000 in the event of a win is a conditional fee—not a contingent fee, which ties the lawyer's payment to the outcome of the case on both the winning *and the award* dimensions (the terminology is not standard, but we think the distinction is useful). Under a contingent-fee contract, the lawyer receives a percentage of the award amount, thus providing an incentive to win and to win big. Unlike conditional fees, contingent fees motivate effort on all margins and are therefore more efficient.[8]

Improved access to the legal system. A second advantage of contingent fees is to improve access to the legal system. Consider what at first seems like a different problem: Imagine that you have a great idea for a new product. Bringing the idea to market will be expensive; you will need to hire engineers, rent office space, enter into distribution agreements, advertise and so forth, and you are not wealthy. You might try to borrow money, but a bank is likely to say that your project is too risky, especially given the bank's limited upside. "Come back when you have some customers," says the bank's lending officer. What you need is a venture capitalist who will supply up-front funds in return for a share of your company. Unlike a bank, the venture capitalist's upside is unlimited, thus enabling him to take significant risks. In addition to funds, the venture capitalist may also bring needed expertise.

A contingent fee-lawyer is a venture capitalist of torts. The contingent-fee lawyer combines a claim with funding and expertise to produce a product to be presented to a judge and jury. Without venture capital, good ideas would lay dormant. Without contingent fees, good cases would lay dormant.

Risk spreading. A closely related point is that venture capital and the contingent fee allow entrepreneurs and plaintiffs to spread some of the risk of their projects to others who are better able to absorb that risk. The plaintiff pays the contingent fee only when he wins and is rich and not when he loses and is poor. Thus, the contingent fee is a form of insurance. Similarly, the contingent fee has aspects of a loan since the lawyer makes his investment early but is not paid until later. These features of contingent fees are desirable to the extent that resource or liquidity constraints might otherwise preclude the litigation of meritorious cases.

Signaling theory. Signaling theory is based on a simple insight: The same contingent fee is more profitable to a high-quality lawyer than to a low-quality lawyer. A lawyer who often wins his cases can afford to offer his services at a contingent fee that would drive a low-quality lawyer out of business. Competition among lawyers pushes the contingent fee down to a level where the high-quality lawyers earn a normal profit and the low-quality lawyers exit the industry. A lawyer who offers to take a case based on hourly fees raises suspicion. Why is this lawyer not willing to work on a contingent-fee basis—is it because he knows that he is unlikely to win the case? Because lawyers' demands for hourly fees send a negative signal, the contingent fee becomes common.[9]

Admittedly, signaling theory seems to prove too much. Patients are at least as uninformed about physician quality as plaintiffs are uninformed about lawyer quality. Why then are contingent fees uncommon in medical care? One response is to argue that this demonstrates a problem in the financing of medical care.[10] We think it more plausible, however, that what makes contingent fees particularly attractive in law is the insurance aspect—the lawyer is paid only when the plaintiff's wealth increases. In other areas where contingent fees might make sense, moral hazard or signaling-type reasons may prevent the adoption of this payoff structure.[11]

Case screening. So-called "screening" theory, a close cousin of signaling theory, elaborates on Elihu Root's observation that "about half of the practice of the decent lawyer consists in telling would-be clients that they are damned fools and should stop" (Glendon 1994).

Suppose you approach a plaintiff's lawyer with a potential case, and he politely declines to represent you on a contingent fee basis: What should you infer? You should infer that the attorney thinks that your case has little chance of winning. Since lawyers are better judges of prospective case outcomes than plaintiffs, this is a useful piece of information. If you cannot get a lawyer to take your case on contingent fee, suing is probably a waste of your time and money.[12]

We should expect contingent-fee lawyers to tell their clients they are fools more often, or at least earlier, than lawyers who are being paid by the hour. Contingent-fee lawyers "screen" potential cases and clients. In constructing a litigation portfolio for his firm, the lawyer will reject weak cases and agree to handle stronger ones. This screening function is useful both for clients and, most likely, for the legal system at large.

CONTINGENT FEES AS A SCREENING DEVICE

It is highly unlikely that caps and other restrictions on contingent-fee arrangements will simply reduce lawyers' earnings. Rather, the effective tax will—like any other tax—prompt dynamic responses, on the part of both lawyers and plaintiffs. These responses may take several forms:

a) Some cases that were profitable for lawyers at a higher contingent fee are no longer profitable at a lower fee. Lawyers now decline these cases.

b) Other cases remain profitable, but because of the lower contingent fees, the income of plaintiff's lawyers declines.

c) Instead of relying on contingent fees, compensation moves toward an hourly fee model.

The case for contingent-fee restrictions rests on the idea that effects (a) and (b) will occur and, moreover, that they are unambiguously beneficial. The possibility of effect (c) is rarely (if ever) acknowledged. That is a crucial mistake.

Assuming that effects (a) and (b) occur, are they actually desirable? On the extreme assumption that most tort cases do not belong in court, *any* reduction in the number of cases is good. But even under this extreme assumption, effect (a) might be small. The cases that are most likely to fall by the wayside as a result of contingent-fee caps are those with a small probability of payoff or a small expected award. By definition, those cases exert only a small effect within the system: Most often they lose, and when they win, the awards are small. Thus, we might not expect big gains from effect (a) even if we make the extreme assumption that most cases do not belong in court. On more moderate assumptions, at least some and perhaps many of the cases that lawyers refuse to take were deserving of compensation, meaning that the overall effect of contingent-fee restrictions is not unambiguously positive. Essentially, *contingent*-fee restrictions would seem to be a haphazard way to eliminate junk lawsuits since they are likely to also eliminate meritorious suits.

As for effect (b), restricting contingent fees may reduce the income of some lawyers, but reducing the income of lawyers *per se* is not a big benefit. So long as large-award cases remain profitable, they will continue to be brought. To the extent that the liabilities are excessive, they will have that effect with or without contingent-fee caps. A million-dollar judgment has the same effect on a physician-defendant regardless of whether the lawyer receives 25 percent or 33 percent of the take. It may stick in some people's craw that contingent-fee lawyers earn a lot of money—in the same way that some people are disturbed when pornographers earn a lot of money. But even if income taxes were higher, Larry Flynt would still be rich and pornography would still be plentiful.

Effect (c) warns us that restricting contingent fees may not reduce lawyer compensation as much as one might first imagine. As restrictions on contingent fees increase, we can expect that noncontingent, or "hourly" fees, as well as other forms of compensation, will become more common. To illustrate the point, consider a more familiar form of the contingent fee: the restaurant tip. Waiters typically earn a large fraction of their income from contingent fees. Suppose that tips were outlawed: What would happen to waiters' wages? Waiters' incomes might decline initially, and waiters might even begin to leave food service for other work, but restaurants would then be forced to raise wages, so that on average waiters earned the same wages with and without tips.

EXIT THE SUPERSTARS?

Our comparison with waiters' tips suggests that contingent-fee caps *might* serve a useful social function by changing the reward amounts and professional incentives of the "superstar" lawyers whose astronomical earnings have played a prominent role in calling attention to contingent fees.

If restaurant owners cannot tell who the very best waiters are, but customers can, the very best waiters will do better with wage and tips compensation than with wage-only compensation. Analogously, capping contingent fees may not reduce lawyer compensation on average, but it could cut into the income of the very best plaintiff's lawyers, unless they can charge for their services in some other manner. As noted, the legal sector of the economy is primarily about redistributing the pie (sometimes justly and sometimes unjustly). As legal fees and other returns to dividing up the pie increase, the returns to growing the pie decrease, and it is possible to get sucked into a downward spiral of poverty creation (Baumol 1990). A well-functioning society, therefore, will seek to ensure that its best and brightest are attracted to professions that create, rather than just redistribute, the wealth.

If liability law helped to create optimal deterrence, the incomes of superstar lawyers would have an efficiency justification. But many of the big cases of the recent past—tobacco, breast implant, and asbestos cases (among many others)—have little or no scientific justification and no demonstrable efficiency gains. Thus, to the extent that contingent-fee caps reduce income of superstar lawyers and thereby encourage them to switch to more productive professions, such caps may prove beneficial.

Although we hold no brief for the superstar lawyers, we are skeptical that fee limits will push many of them out of the profession. Julia Roberts would still make millions, and still be an actress, even if she never took a cut of the box office receipts. Superstar lawyers would still be superstar lawyers even if contingent fees were capped. We can expect similar forces to unfold in the legal industry: In the long run, serious restrictions on contingent fees will encourage alternative payment systems. Even today, such alternatives are readily available. Plaintiff's lawyers use multiple sources of compensation, primarily contingent fees, but also fees for expert witnesses and other trial preparation costs (Cumming 2001, 258). Contingent-fee caps would likely produce a shift in that direction.

Perhaps most obviously, the contingent fee could also be replaced by a *conditional fee*. (As explained, a conditional fee is an outcome-dependent form of compensation that is topped off in the event of a win—for example, zero dollars if the plaintiff loses, $50,000 if he wins.) Conditional fees, which are common in other countries, are not regulated under the current laws limiting contingent fees. Of course, contingent-fee restrictions could be extended to conditional fees as well. In that event, though, the capitalization and insurance functions of contingent fees would likely be provided by third-parties. Some such arrangements, too, already exist. LawCash, for example, lends money to plaintiffs to pay their legal fees or other expenses. The loan is paid off (with a steep fee) only if the plaintiff recovers in a settlement or trial.[13] Similarly, legal insurance will become more common if plaintiffs cannot rely on the contingent fee. Lawyers might even begin to work for fixed fees in LMOs, Legal Maintenance Organizations, analogous to HMOs in the healthcare industry. In short: Contingent fee-arrangements are common because they bundle various functions that are useful for both lawyers and plaintiffs. Contingent-fee caps will, at the limit and in the long run, force an unbundling of these functions. There is no reason to believe that the resulting industry structures will be more efficient than contingent fees. Currently, for example, third-party loans and legal insurance operate largely as backstops to the prevailing contingent-fee practice, which suggests that they are *less* desirable.

At the same time, contingent-fee caps threaten to compromise the screening function of contingent fees by pushing parties into substituting the most obvious financing alternative—the hourly fee. The screening theory suggests that as lawyers increase their reliance on hourly fees, they will be more willing to take weaker cases. Why not, when the client is paying by the hour? This prediction is sufficiently important to merit empirical examination.

In principle, one could examine whether cases taken under the hourly fee win less often than cases taken under the contingent fee. The difficulty with this procedure, however, is that cases taken to trial are not a random sample of all cases (Priest and Klein 1984,1–2). The nonrandom character of trials makes it questionable to look at win rates directly. For that reason, we test a related implication of the screening theory. As time passes and cases move through the legal system, clients gain information. With better information, some of the plaintiffs with weak cases will realize that they are unlikely to win and in consequence they will drop their cases. In other words, some of the hourly fee clients with weak cases will learn what a contingent-fee lawyer would have told them on day one, and they then drop their cases, wiser but poorer.

We tested this hypothesis through an analysis of case outcomes in various states with *and without* contingent-fee caps in different classes of cases. We drew our data from the *Civil Justice Survey of State Courts, 1992*, a survey of litigation conducted by the U.S. Department of Justice and the Bureau of Justice Statistics.[14] Currently, sixteen states limit the contingent fees that lawyers may charge in medical malpractice cases (American Medical Association 1989, and Table 1). Of the sixteen states that have limits, ten have counties in the State Court data set. Two states, Florida and Michigan, limit contingent fees in all personal injury cases, which makes it difficult to create an in-state control group. Therefore, we drop Florida and Michigan from the analysis. All of the remaining states limit contingent fees in medical malpractice cases but not in auto cases. Thus constructed, we have eight "hourly fee" states (i.e., states with limits on contingent fees in medical malpractice cases but not in auto cases). These states are California, Connecticut, Illinois, Indiana, Massachusetts, New Jersey, New York, and Wisconsin. There are also eight "contingent fee" states (*i.e.*, states without limits in any class of case); these states are Georgia, Kentucky, Minnesota, Missouri, Ohio, Pennsylvania, Texas, and Virginia. Table 1 shows the distribution.

The adoption of contingent-fee caps in selected states allows us to examine data from a sample of tort cases to test whether plaintiffs drop their cases more often in states that restrict contingent fees. As a first step, we examine exclusively medical malpractice cases. Table 2 shows that in states without limits on contingent fees, just under 5 percent of medical malpractice cases are dropped. In contrast, in states *with* limits, a whopping 18 percent of medical malpractice cases are dropped.

States with and without limits on contingent fees could differ in ways other than fee limits. To test whether other factors account for the difference in drop rates, we take advantage of the fact that many states have restricted contingent fees in medical malpractice cases but not in other types of cases. When we apply this "difference-in-the-differences" analysis, we find that drop rates in automobile cases are nearly identical in states that do and do not restrict contingent fees in medical malpractice cases (9.7 percent vs. 10.2 percent). Thus, across the same set of states, we find big differences in drop rates in cases where contingent fees are limited, but no such differences in cases that have no such restrictions.

In our earlier work, we further controlled for a variety of other variables, such as the type of defendant, the type of plaintiff claim, and caps on punitive damages. Using the same difference-in-the-differences technique in a more sophisticated econometric model called

TABLE I.

State	Limits	Effective Dates	Actions to which limit applies	In State Courts Data
California	40% of first $50,000 33⅓% of the next $50,000 25% of the next $500,000 15% of damages that exceed $600,000	1975	Medical Malpractice	Yes
Connecti-cut	33⅓% of first $300,000 25% of the next $300,000 20% of the next $300,000 15% of the next $300,000 10% of the next $300,000	1986	Medical Malpractice	Yes
Delaware	Unclear	1976	Medical Malpractice	No
Florida	33⅓% of any recovery up to $1 million through the time of filing of an answer or the demand for appointment of arbitrators 40% of any recovery up to $1 million through the trial of the case 30% of any recovery between $1 million and $2 million 20% of any recovery in excess of $2 million	1985 (Nov.)	Medical Malpractice Cases (extended to all personal injury cases in 1986)	Yes
Illinois	33⅓% of the first $150,000 25% of the next $850,000 20% of amounts over $1,000,000	1985	Medical Malpractice	Yes
Maine	33⅓% of the first $100,000 25% of the next $100,000 20% of amounts over $200,000	1986	Medical Malpractice	No
New Jersey	33 1/3% of the first $250,000 25% of the next $250,000 20% of the next $500,000 if the award exceeds $1,000,000 the attorney must apply to the assignment judge for a higher fee	1976	All Personal Injury Cases	Yes

TABLE I. (*cont.*)

State	Limits	Effective Dates	Actions to which limit applies	In State Courts Data
New York	30% of the first $250,000 25% of the next $250,000 20% of the next $500,000 15% of the next $250,000 10% of any amount over $1,250,000	1976	Medical Malpractice	Yes
Wisconsin	33⅓% of the first $250,000 25% of the first $1,000,000 depending when the case is settled. 20% of over $1,000,000	1986	Medical Malpractice	Yes
Indiana	15% of any recovery from the compensation fund	1975	Workers Compensation	Yes
Michigan	33⅓% of any award	1981	All Personal Injury Cases	Yes
Nevada	40% of the first $50,000, 33⅓% of the next $50,000, 25% of the next $500,000 and 15% of everything over $600,000.	2005	Medical Malpractice	No
Oklahoma	50% of any award	1953	All Personal Injury Cases	No
Oregon	⅓ of the amount received and 20% of punitive damages	1995	Medical Malpractice	No
Tennessee	⅓ with court review	1975	Medical Malpractice	No
Utah	33⅓% of all awards	1985	Medical Malpractice	No

Source: Brannon (1997).

a probit model, we find results that are very similar to the simpler test presented here.

The test in Table 2 uses data from across the states during the same period of time. A complementary test uses data from the same state at different points in time. Florida limited contingent fees in medical malpractice cases in November of 1985. We therefore looked at drop rates before and after November of 1985. The shorter the before and after periods examined, the more confident we can be that other factors remained the same. Accordingly, we compared the drop rate of cases filed 300 days before the contingent-fee limits were imposed with the drop rate filed in the 300 days after the limits took effect. Table 3 shows the results.[15]

Once again, we find that drop rates increased after contingent fees were restricted. The increase in drops is 3.5 percentage points or approximately a 15 percent increase. While the increase in dropped cases is smaller than that observed in the cross-state regressions, recall that the increase here occurred within less than a year from the time contingent fees were imposed.

Our results provide indirect evidence for our contention that contingent-fee restrictions erode screening and increase the proportion of low-value suits within the system.

TABLE 2 Proportion of Dropped Cases in Fee Limit and Non-Limit States (State Courts Data).

		Total Cases	Dropped Cases	Proportion
States with Limits on Contingent Fees (Hourly Fee States)	Medical Malpractice	454	83	18.3%[***]
	Auto	4,838	468	9.7%
Non-Limit States	Medical Malpractice	287	14	4.9%[***]
	Auto	3,474	353	10.2%

***The difference between these two percentages is statistically significant at the greater than 1% level.

TABLE 3 Proportion of Dropped Cases Pre and Post 1985 Limit (Florida Data).

Period	Total Cases	Dropped Cases	Proportion
Pre-Limits (1985)	1,938	440	22.7%[**]
Post-Limits (1985–1986)	1,064	279	26.2%[**]

**Difference is statistically significant at the 5% level.

UNEQUAL INCENTIVES?

Contingent fees are often said to drive a wedge between the client's and the representing lawyer's interests when it comes to settling a case. Unequal incentives have been said to affect settlement rates and values as well as the time to settlement. These assertions are difficult to refute or to confirm. Economic models of the settlement process are highly sensitive to the underlying assumptions, and empirical studies are sparse and inconclusive. Our own studies find no evidence that contingent fees affect settlement rates one way or the other. We do, however, find evidence that contingent fees reduce the time to settlement.

Settlement rates. The basic argument is that under a contingent fee, the lawyer bears all the costs of litigation but receives only a fraction of the benefits. On the margin, then, the lawyer has a greater incentive to settle than the client.[16] At the outset, it is important to put this (perceived or real) asymmetry and its potential effects into context. At a two-thirds client and one-third lawyer split, the plaintiff's interests and the lawyer's interests differ only by a factor of 2—far smaller than in other contexts, such as real estate transactions, where contingent fees are common.

More importantly, one must avoid what Harold Demsetz called the "Nirvana fallacy" (Demsetz 1969). A comparison of the actual to the ideal is bound to be unflattering to the actual. The relevant alternative to the contingent fee is not the "efficient solution" as found in an economic model with complete information. The relevant alternative is the hourly fee or perhaps the less often used flat fee. Under the hourly fee, the lawyer has too little incentive to settle—after all, settling means the end of payments for the lawyer. And, as noted above, a lawyer's effort is likely to be too low under the hourly fee. Compared to that massive asymmetry of incentives (and the exorbitant monitoring costs required to curtail its effects), the divergence of interests under contingent fees are bound to be limited.

It is also unclear which ways those asymmetries cut. The argument that under-incentivized lawyers will "sell out" their clients assumes that the lawyer has control over a pending settlement. If control over a settlement remains with the client, it is easy to turn the argument around. Under contingent fees, the client is less interested in settling than under hourly fees, because the costs of the trial are born principally by the lawyer. Moreover, knowing that plaintiffs face few of the costs of going to trial can encourage defendants to settle. Thus, the net effect on settlement is not obvious.

Even if we assume that the lawyers have considerable control over whether or not to settle, reputation and the demand for repeat business will induce lawyers to settle as their clients would wish. Lawyers do not want to have a reputation for settling too easily, and they do want to have a reputation for producing good results for their clients. Repeat business and business from friends and family are important for most lawyers (Kritzer 2002).

Finally, clients have a number of available means to motivate the lawyer to settle optimally. If the lawyer has too great an incentive to settle, for example, then it's a simple matter to raise the contingent fee if the case goes to trial (for example, 25 percent if settled before trial and 33 percent if the case goes to trial). Alternatively, if the problem is that the lawyer bears all the costs but receives only a fraction of the benefits, a solution is for the client to bear some of the costs. If the lawyer reaps one-third of the benefits and bears one-third of the burden, for example, then his incentive to settle will be exactly the same as his client's. Such an expense-sharing scheme would usually require payment of some up-front costs on the part of the client, although modifications can eliminate this necessity, too.[17] While financing plans of this sort are rarely explicit, it is not uncommon for clients to bear some of the costs of prosecuting a case (Cumming 2001). Empirical evidence on the effect on contingent fees for settlement rates is quite limited. An ideal study would compare outcomes of cases that were randomly assigned to contingent- or to hourly-fees lawyers. No such study exists, however, and only a few (and now somewhat dated) studies have examined the question at all.

- In a 1991 study, Terry Thomason found that plaintiffs who hire lawyers have higher settlement rates and lower settlement amounts than plaintiffs who represent themselves. Because lawyers in these cases are paid at least some of their compensation from a contingent-fee arrangement, Thomason concludes that contingent fees *increase* settlement rates and *reduce* settlement amounts (Thomason 1991, 218). Two reasons suggest caution before accepting these conclusions. First, self-selection is potentially an important factor when some plaintiffs choose to hire lawyers and others do not. If plaintiffs who hire lawyers have weaker cases (a plausible assumption), we might expect settlement rates in this group to be higher and settlement amounts to be lower. Second, even assuming that selection effects are absent, Thomason cannot distinguish whether the effects he finds are due to representation by lawyers or to lawyer fee arrangements.

- A second piece of evidence on the impact of contingent fees is found in Patricia Danzon and Lee Lillard's model of dispute resolution. Although contingent fees are not the focus of their investigation, Danzon and Lillard estimate the effect of restrictions of contingent fees on settlement rates. (Their data cover 1974 and 1976, allowing them to pick up a number of law changes which occurred in 1975.) They find that restrictions on contingent fees are associated with a 1.5 percentage point *increase* in the settlement rate (Danzon and Lillard 1983, 363).

- From a survey of lawyers, Douglas Cumming finds that disputes over settlement between lawyer and client occur *less* often when the lawyer charges using a contingent fee (Cumming 2001, 270). One has to be wary of survey results on disputes, as lawyers may not wish to advertise how many client disputes that they have had. Still, the result is inconsistent with the notion that contingent fees separate the interests of lawyer and client.

Thus, the existing research, including our own, does not provide robust, clear-cut results regarding the effect of contingency fees on settlement rates.

Time to settlement. Changing the time to settlement is different from changing the probability of settlement. Longer times, for example, could be associated with higher or lower probabilities of settlement. Longer times to settlement could be associated with a higher probability of settlement if, for example, extra time allows for more settlements; longer times could be associated with lower settlement probabilities if, for example, the extended time bumps more cases against the trial date.

Contingent fees have been accused of both slowing down the time to settlement and speeding up the time to settlement. In an influential critique of contingent fees, for example, Walter Olson has argued that

> [m]ost litigants tire of their fights, if not at first, then after a while, and at some point would rather get on with their lives than hold out for a little more. The lawyer with a big war chest has an incentive to make you wait in order to go for the extra money (Olson 1991).

On the other hand, David Bernstein has claimed that "[b]ecause time is most definitely money in the legal business, it pays the contingent-fee attorney to settle as quickly as possible . . . " (Bernstein 1996).

We suspect that the latter theory is more likely to be correct on average. An hourly fee lawyer has a greater incentive to rack up hours than one on contingent fee and this will tend to increase the time to settlement. (This is *not* true by definition: It is easy to delay settling a case without working many hours.) Thus, when contingent fees are restricted and a higher proportion of lawyer remuneration comes from hourly fees, we expect that cases will take longer to be settled. Of course, an hourly fee lawyer will not be paid for pure delay, but by spending more time on discovery, searching for legal precedents, beginning with unattractive settlement bids, and encouraging clients to refuse early settlement offers, a lawyer can increase the time to settlement *and* billable hours.

Using the State Courts and Florida data sets described earlier, we estimate the effect of restricting contingent fees on the expected time until settlement. As before, we take into account other factors using auto cases as a control. We also use a number of other control variables under a censored Tobit regression on the log of settlement time (Helland and Tabarrok 2003). In the State Courts data, we find that restricting contingent fees increases the time to settlement by 22 percent. Similarly, we find that in the 13 months after contingent fees were restricted in medical malpractice cases in Florida, the time to settlement increased by 13 percent.

Thus, we find little evidence that contingent fees markedly increase settlement rates. We do find that restrictions on contingent fees increase the time to settlement and also increase the number cases that plaintiffs waste time filing but eventually drop.

DO CONTINGENT FEES YIELD EXCESS RETURNS TO LAWYERS?

If contingent fees are part of an optimum plaintiff-lawyer client contract, why is it that contingent-fee lawyers seem to earn "excessive" returns? Lester Brickman, for example, a leading critic of contingent fees, has claimed that

> [c]ontingent-fee lawyers have not only flouted ethical rules and fiducial protections but have also imposed substantial rents on tort claimants as the price for tort claiming ... contingent-fee lawyers generate substantial rents and obtain inordinately high rates of return, not infrequently amounting to thousands and even tens of thousands of dollars an hour (Brickman 2003).

Certainly, one can find examples of very high payments to contingent-fee lawyers. Most of these, however, involve either class actions or cases that are altogether *sui generis*. As mentioned earlier, in 1998 a group of lawyers was awarded over $8.2 *billion* in fees for representing Florida, Mississippi, and Texas in their suits against tobacco companies to recover healthcare expenses. All told, the state settlements generated somewhere between $18 billion and $38 billion in fees, equivalent to tens of thousands of dollars per hour in compensation for each lawyer involved. But while the fees in the tobacco deal have become a mainstay of contingent-fee critics, that deal was less a settlement of a legal case than a political bargain between the tobacco companies, the state governments, and the lawyers, all of whom gained at the expense of an unrepresented group, the smokers. The fees are shocking; but then, so was the tobacco deal itself. Lower fees would hardly have made the deal more reasonable.

Similarly, contingent fees in class actions are by no means representative of all lawyer-client contracts. Plaintiffs in class actions often do not know a suit is even being brought on their behalf (Hensler 2001, 190). Judicial review of these settlements is required because plaintiffs have little incentive to monitor "their" attorneys. [18]

To evaluate the fees in contingent fee cases, we need to look at more run-of-the-mill cases. With respect to those cases, little if any empirical evidence buttresses the contention that contingent-fee lawyers earn above-normal returns, and standard economic theory provides potent reasons for skepticism that such returns could be sustained for any length of time.

Contingent fees, ex ante and ex post. In part, the outrage over contingent fees represents a case of mistaking what is seen for all that is. After a case has been settled or concluded, contingent fees may appear large relative to the hours a lawyer has put into that particular case, but the fee needs to be evaluated ex ante—that is, before the case begins. Consider the simplest possible example. Assume that there is a one-half probability that a case will be won and if won damages will be equal to $15,000 with certainty. Assume that the contingent fee is set at one-third, and that the lawyer puts ten hours of work into the case. If the case is won, the lawyer receives $5,000 or $500 per hour—quite a high hourly fee. But recall that the case wins one-half of the time, the other half of the time, the lawyer receives nothing, so the expected hourly fee is $250 (not bad, but that is before expenses). More generally, if the appropriate hourly fee is $X per hour we can expect the equivalent hourly fee calculated from winnings to be $X/p where p is the probability of winning. If the probability of winning is one-half, we can expect the equivalent hourly fee in contingent-fee cases to be twice as high as a regular hourly fee. If the case is particularly unlikely to succeed, the equivalent hourly fee may be much higher.

Most cases are settled rather than tried, but the same principle applies when we consider that settlement amounts are uncertain. Assume that the damages in a given case are uncertain—say, a 50 percent probability of $25,000 and a 50 percent probability of $5,000. In some winning cases, the equivalent hourly fee will be $833, but in others, just $166. The expected equivalent hourly fee is identical to that found earlier, but *ex post*, it will appear that in some cases the fees were exorbitant, a veritable rip-off. Yet we know that the ex-ante fee was reasonable. Add to the mix some small probabilities of very large awards, and it is easy to see how equivalent hourly fees may appear huge even when expected hourly fees do not depart greatly from regular hourly fees. Recall our earlier analogy to venture capitalists. It is common to hear about venture capitalists who multiply their investment ten or even one hundred times, but those huge returns are paralleled by many investments that return little or nothing.

Equivalence or collusion? Brickman claims that even in ordinary cases, contingent-fee lawyers earn excessive and unjustifiable returns. But Brickman's evidence is primarily anecdotal and is contradicted by more substantial data (see further below). The argument that contingent-fee lawyers are earning substantial excess returns is inconsistent with basic economic theory and the fact of extensive competition in the market for lawyers. If contingent-fee lawyers were, "not infrequently" earning thousands or tens of thousands of dollars an hour, they would be earning far more than hourly fee lawyers (i.e., defense lawyers and corporate lawyers). That seems highly unlikely. Plaintiff and defense lawyers have very similar amounts of education and skill, so we would expect them to have similar earnings. If contingent-fee lawyers were earning markedly higher fees than defense lawyers, the defense lawyers would switch practice until earnings were equalized. In short, we expect to see roughly equivalent returns for hourly and contingent-fee lawyers, with some adjustments being made for insurance and interest payments and due allowance being made for a handful of contingent-fee superstars.

Empirical evidence is consistent with these expectations. Herbert Kritzer surveyed Wisconsin lawyers and found a median hourly fee of $125 and an equivalent hourly fee for those lawyers on contingent fee of $132. As expected, a handful of cases from a handful of lawyers were very profitable on an hourly basis, so mean figures showed larger differences with a mean hourly fee of $124 per hour and an equivalent hourly fee of $242. Kritzer found similar ranges in a data set of federal cases (Kritzer 2002, 765 and 1998, 275). Due to the difficulties of measuring and controlling for factors such as case type, quality of lawyer, hours, insurance, and interest payments, we should not put too much weight on these precise findings. Certainly, however, the data provide no evidence of "abuse" or "extortionate" practices in contingent-fee pricing. They are fully consistent with the roughly equivalent returns that are predicted by economic reasoning.

Brickman has argued that contingent-fee lawyers collude to maintain higher equivalent hourly fees (Brickman 2003a, 699–703 and 2003b). While it is certainly true that due to restrictions on entry, the market for lawyers is not fully competitive, those barriers work to raise the earnings of *all* lawyers. It is one thing to claim that lawyers earn more because they have managed to exclude competition from paralegals; it is quite another to assert that one type of lawyer earns more than other types of lawyers, despite the fact that no entry barrier prevents a lawyer from changing his pricing scheme at the drop of a hat.

In support of a collusion theory, Brickman and others observe and inveigh against the fact that the same contingent fee applies to a big case as to a small case (Brickman 2003a and 2003b). The suggestion here is that time and effort do not rise in direct proportion to the "size" of a case. If a one-third contingent fee for small cases is competitive, then—the argument runs—the same fee for a big case must be supra-competitive, and the prevalence of that fee structure must be due to collusion. But that is a *non sequitur*. While it is possible, though difficult, to believe that the market for lawyers is uncompetitive, we observe very similar pricing and compensation patterns in markets that are clearly and almost pristinely competitive. Again, it is useful to compare contingent fees in law with contingent fees for waiters. Here, the same 15 percent to 20 percent tip applies to expensive restaurants as to cheap restaurants. It is unlikely in the extreme, however, that waiters collude to maintain tip percentages or that waiters at expensive restaurants rip off the customers. A more likely explanation is that waiters at expensive restaurants are better waiters. (One interesting piece of evidence in support of this theory is that waiters at expensive restaurants are typically paid higher wages *in addition* to earning far more in tips.) For analogous reasons, high-quality lawyers will be in a better position than less-qualified lawyers to assemble a portfolio of high-value cases with better-than-average chances of prevailing. The uniformity of contingent-fee arrangements *in percentage terms* is more likely to reflect these demand-driven dynamics than is collusion.

CONTINGENT FEES AND THE SOCIAL INTEREST

Clients watch out for their own interests. Not every client is capable of well-guarding their interests in every transaction, of course, but as with other markets, competition is the consumer's best friend and lawyers do sell their services in competitive markets. Claims that the contingent fee harms the interests of clients, therefore, should be regarded with some suspicion at least to the extent of requiring strong evidence. But we have found no strong evidence that contingent fees harm the interests of clients. On the contrary, we have found evidence that restrictions on contingent fees contribute to wasted plaintiff effort (as evidenced by dropped cases) and longer times to settlement.

Contingent fees, however, may harm social interests even as they contribute to plaintiff interests. We have good grounds for thinking that competition promotes the interests of buyers, but competition alone is no guarantee that the interests of society will be promoted. Competition among hit-men benefits the buyers of their services, but not society at large. Walter Olson makes this argument for contingent fees:

> The case against the contingent fee has always rested on the danger it poses not to the one who pays it but to the opponent and more widely to justice itself. As other nations recognize, it can yoke together lawyer and client in a perfectly harmonious and efficient assault on the general public. There are things lawyers will do when a fortune for themselves is on the line that they won't do when it's just a fortune for a client ... Giving soldiers contingent fees for successful attacks, by letting them loot the town they capture, was long favored as a way of encouraging warlike zeal but came under gradual ethical control as civilization progressed ... Giving lawyers contingent fees encourages similar abuses of both the client and the public (Olson 1991).

We offer a rough test of the Olson thesis (which, it bears mention, runs counter to Brickman's theory of contingent fees as a conspiracy against the client). We examine whether awards are lower when contingent fees are restricted. Again, using data from the *Civil Justice Survey of State Courts, 1992*, we find that awards in the states that limit contingent fees are more than twice as high as in states without restrictions. The results are shown in Table 4 below. The raw data show the exact opposite result to that hypothesized by opponents of contingent fees.

We caution, however, that the data need to be taken with several grains of salt. We have not controlled for other factors that may account for differences across the states. A simple first step is to examine auto awards in these same states. Again, the results appear in Table 4. Awards are also higher in auto cases (which are not limited by contingent-fee caps) in states that limit contingent fees in medical malpractice cases, but the difference in awards remains large even after taking this into account. That is, the ratio between mean medical-malpractice awards and mean automobile awards is higher in states that restrict contingency fees in medical-malpractice cases than it is in states with no restrictions.

That result, to repeat, should not be over-interpreted. We have taken no account of "reverse causality"—that is, of the possibility that states with large medical malpractice awards are more likely to

TABLE 4 Restrictions on Contingent Fees Do Not Appear to Reduce Awards in Medical Malpractice Cases.

	Mean Award	Observations
Medical Malpractice Cases in Fee Limit States	$500,816	327
Medical Malpractice Cases in No Limit States	$225,105	313
Auto Cases in Limit States	$173,886	708
Auto Cases in No Limit States	$99,119	954

Source: Civil Justice Survey of State Courts, 1992

pass limits on contingent fees than other states—and of other complicating and confounding factors. A more thorough analysis must await another day. Our purpose in presenting the data is simply to make the *prima facie* argument that restricting contingent fees does not greatly reduce awards.

Another common criticism of contingent fees is that they promote "excessive," "speculative," or "frivolous" litigation, to use three terms found in the literature. Bernstein (1996), for example, writes that the contingent fee "encourages attorneys to engage in speculative litigation in the hope of landing the occasional large jackpot." Our results on contingent fees and dropped cases, however, indicates that it is the hourly fee that encourages attorneys to bring frivolous litigation, understood as cases that are unlikely to win.

More generally, many tort reforms have been motivated by the view that contingent fees increase the number of cases that do not belong in the courts. The exact reasoning behind this claim is not always clear. Two ideas need to be distinguished. If contingent fees help plaintiffs overcome risk aversion or capital constraints, one would expect contingent fees to increase the *amount* of litigation. Critics of contingent fees tend to be critics of the tort system in general so this effect alone is enough to make them condemn contingent fees.

If the problem to be solved is too many cases in the courts, then the appropriate solution is a congestion fee. Why interfere in the contracting of plaintiffs and lawyers, reducing their opportunities for risk-sharing and -borrowing, when a more direct solution is possible? Alternatively, perhaps the problem is that awards are too high or are granted in cases where they should not be granted. There is mounting evidence that this is the case. The tort system in 2002 comprised an estimated 2.23 percent of GDP.[19] Yet this vast and expensive system is not particularly accurate. For example, a Harvard study of New York hospitalization injuries (resulting from hospitalizations in 1984) found that half of the medical-malpractice awards arose from instances where neither negligence nor any identifiable injury occurred and one-third arose from instances in which the patient was injured but the doctor was not negligent (e.g., a previously unknown drug allergy). Only one-sixth of the cases identified instances of true negligence as identified by an independent panel. Yet the vast majority of these cases received compensation.[20] The results were similar in a study covering Utah and Colorado hospitalizations in 1992 (Studdert and Brennan 2000). Viewed in this way, one might argue that if most cases are without merit, any reform that reduced them is an improvement.

However, the studies also found that 3 percent to 4 percent of hospitalizations appear to give rise to adverse events, such as drug reactions, and that approximately one-third to one-half of these adverse events are due to negligent actions. In short, few injured people sue, and relatively few suits involve injured people. The problem is not how lawyers are paid, but that the court system does not do a good job of screening meritless cases.

It is quite appropriate to draw attention to factors such as elected judges, jury demographics, and perhaps most importantly, bad law that unfairly and inefficiently drives awards skyward, but these root causes of higher awards have little do with contingent fees. Tort reform is desirable, but the problems of inefficient lawsuits are better addressed directly, with changes in the law, rather than with restrictions on how lawyers are paid.

Blaming contingent fees for out-of-control courts is like blaming credit cards for personal bankruptcy. It's not that there is no connection between credit cards and personal bankruptcy, but it's easy enough to go bankrupt without a credit card. There are many benefits of credit cards and we would not want arbitrarily to dissuade credit card use (Zywicki 2000, 166–170). Similarly, the connection between contingent fees and out-of-control courts may not be zero, but restricting contingent fees is a poor way of reining in the courts.

Instead, the evidence from the studies of medical-malpractice cases strongly suggests that reforms should aim at improving the judicial screening system to prevent meritless cases.

CONCLUSION: TORT REFORM BY PROXY?

Contingent fees have a number of benefits, such as helping to motivate lawyers, even when clients find it difficult to monitor their lawyers. Contingent fees also force lawyers to be honest with their clients about the quality of the client's case. A contingent-fee lawyer will not take on a case that he expects to lose. As a result, we hypothesize that restrictions on contingent fees will increase, not decrease, the number of low-quality suits as hourly fee lawyers take on cases that a contingent-fee lawyer would reject. Using dropped cases as a measure of quality, we find that clients drop their cases much more often when the use of contingent fees is limited. The result is robust. We find that restrictions on contingent fees increase dropped cases using two different data sets, one that examines differences across the states at a single point in time and another that looks at a single state across a period of time. In both cases, we are able to use differences in auto cases, where contingent fees are not limited, as a control variable.

Contingency fee restrictions appear to be a blunt and potentially ineffective way to reform the tort system. As discussed here, there is very little evidence that contingency fee restrictions eliminate a substantial proportion of frivolous lawsuits, and theory, along with some empirical evidence, suggests that limiting contingency fees actually increases a plaintiff attorney's incentives to pursue low-quality cases. Supporters of tort reform would be better served by pursuing other avenues that have more potential to improve social welfare.

6

Conclusions and Options for Reform

In Chapter 1, we surveyed evidence showing that the tort system is an expensive method of compensating victims for their injuries. We also noted that the current evidence does not show that the tort system deters injuries by enough to offset these costs. In subsequent chapters, we have focused on three hot spots—juries, particularly poor, minority juries, but also juries in general as compared to judges; partisan-elected judges; and contingency fees. Surprisingly, given the bad press that lawyers have received, we do not think that reform of contingency fees is an especially useful reform. High lawyer income is an effect of bad law more than a cause of bad law.

It is tempting to conclude from our findings, however, that juries and partisan-elected judges are a problem where the solution is more appointed judges. But some cautions are in order. Juries and elected judges need to be evaluated within the entire context of the American legal system. We have only examined the effect of these institutions on tort awards and have said little about, for example, criminal trials, Federal-State relations, or constitutional issues. The founders thought the jury trial was important enough to be guaranteed in the Bill of Rights. Why? The founders were impressed with the jury as a form of check and balance against oppressive government.

On August 5, 1735, twelve New York jurors, inspired by the eloquence of the best lawyer of the period, Andrew Hamilton, ignored the instructions of the Governor's handpicked judges and returned a verdict of "Not Guilty" on the charge of publishing "seditious libels." The Zenger trial is a remarkable story of a divided Colony, the beginnings of a free press, and the stubborn independence of American jurors.[1]

Since that time, juries have continued to be one force keeping the law in the hands of the people. Juries, for example, have refused at times to convict for violations of the fugitive slave laws, prohibition, and the draft. We hypothesize that elected judges may function somewhat like juries in keeping power close to the people. Juries and elected judges, of course, have also abused their powers. We do not intend to resolve these debates here, but only to draw attention to some of the larger issues that an excessive focus on torts may obscure.

Although we are reluctant to suggest radical change, we do think that marginal change may be justified. But appropriate reforms require an understanding of the real problem to be addressed. To that end, it's worthwhile to ask again why partisan-elected judges and some juries grant much higher awards than others. The problem, in fact, may not be elected judges and juries *per se*! Recall that our primary finding concerning partisan-elected judges was not that awards are higher in states that use partisan elections to select their judges, but that awards against *out-of-state defendants* were much higher in these states. Here, once again, is how retired West Virginia Richard Neely explained his incentives:

> As long as I am allowed to redistribute wealth from out-of-state companies to injured in-state plaintiffs, I shall continue to do so. Not only is my sleep enhanced when I give someone else's money away, but so is my job security, because the in-state plaintiffs, their families, and their friends will reelect me (Neely 1988, 4).

But now consider our finding that awards are much higher in counties with a lot of minority poverty. Almost by definition, the largest defendants in cases filed in poor, minority-dominated counties are companies headquartered out-of-county and probably out-of-state. It's quite plausible, therefore, that both the partisan-electoral and the poverty effect are driven in large part by redistribution incentives.

It's important to recall that the original idea of the jury was to draw jurors from the community in which the crime or tort occurred because these were the individuals most informed about the event: Local juries were to judge local events. Today, however, we have in many cases reversed this formula: Local juries judge events on a national and even an international scale.

Garvey v. Roto-Rooter Services Co. is a class-action case filed in Madison County, Illinois.[2] The single Madison County resident named in the suit is suing "on behalf" of customers of Roto-Rooter in thirty other states. The complaint does not allege a defect in service, but instead that the individuals performing the service were not licensed plumbers. Put aside the concern that many economists, not to mention consumers, would consider the resulting lower prices a blessing, and consider the absurdity that a judge and jury from Madison County, Illinois, will in effect be deciding plumbing laws and regulation for thirty other states. Not surprisingly, judges in Madison County are elected.

Or consider *Avery v. State Farm Mutual Auto Insurance*. In this case, the local plaintiff complained, on behalf of all State Farm consumers nationwide, that State Farm had acted deceptively by refusing to provide original equipment manufacturer (OEM) parts to policy-holders involved in car accidents.[3] A jury awarded the class more than $1 billion. The case is especially galling because several insurance commissioners from other states testified that such a ruling would contravene their own laws that encouraged and sometimes even required non-OEM parts in order to lower insurance costs.

Class-action cases like these can be decided in state court only because of an anomaly in federal law. The Constitution provides that cases between citizens of different states be decided by federal judges, but in implementing this constitutional requirement, Congress and the courts decided that a case would be subject to federal diversity jurisdiction only if there was "complete diversity"—every defendant had to be an out-of-state defendant.[4] As a result, it becomes quite easy to "defeat diversity" by suing a local defendant. In Jefferson County, Mississippi, for example, the Bankston Drug Store has been sued hundreds of time—not because the pharmacy did anything wrong, but simply as a way to defeat diversity in lawsuits against out-of-state pharmaceutical manufacturers.

Keeping the amount in controversy below $75,000 can also defeat diversity. Unfortunately, this common-sense provision has been interpreted to mean that so long as none of the plaintiffs, numbering possibly in the millions, asks for more than $75,000, the case can be kept in state court even if it involves millions of dollars in total (Beisner and Miller 2001).

Some of the defects in 28 USC S. 1332 have been remedied by the Class Action Fairness Act (CAFA), first introduced into Congress in 1999. CAFA requires federal diversity jurisdiction if the class has at least one hundred plaintiffs and damages exceed an aggregate of $5 million. CAFA is a modest step in the right direction toward tort reform. It is especially appropriate, we believe, because as compared with other, cruder reforms, it is consistent with American legal tradition. The framers of the U.S. Constitution gave federal judges control over cases between citizens of different states precisely because they feared that local courts would use their powers unfairly against out-of-state defendants (Friendly 1928). In 2000, a Senate Report on the CAFA emphasized this point:

> Clearly, a system that allows State court judges to dictate national policy from the local courthouse steps is contrary to

the intent of the Framers, when they crafted our system of federalism.[5]

Forum choice is suggestive of the steps that need to be taken but is not the solution alone. The research presented in this book suggests that meaningful tort reform results from removing from juries or judges cases in which they do not have the proper incentives or the capacity to decide cases objectively. Unless we are willing to construct an alternative compensation system for injuries, as was done with workers' compensation systems early in the last century, meaningful reform will take two paths. Either it will limit the decision-making power of judges or juries by statute, or it will allow private parties to impose such limits by contract.

LIMITATIONS ON JUDGES AND JURIES BY STATUTE

Limiting the power of judges and juries by statute has been the preferred method of tort reform since the mid-1970s. We are skeptical of such blunt instruments as damage caps, although caps on damages for pain and suffering may have merit (see Rubin 1993). The difficulty is not that such reforms do not work, but that they do not address the underlying problems. The tort system does a poor job of selecting those cases in which a doctor has been negligent, and it often compensates those who have not been negligently injured. Limiting damages may prevent a bad system from hemorrhaging, but it would be better if the hemorrhaging could be prevented in the first place.

Our research suggests that more subtle statutory limitations on the decision-making power of judges and juries can be more effective. The courts, for example, have become much less tolerant of junk science than they were in the past. Huber (1991) stated the problem well:

Junk science is impelled through our courts by a mix of opportunity and incentive. "Let-it-all-in" legal theory creates the opportunity. The incentive is money: the prospect that the Midas-like touch of a credulous jury will now and again transform scientific dust into gold. Ironically, the law's tolerance for pseudoscientific speculation has been rationalized in the name of science itself. The open-minded traditions of science demanded that every claim be taken seriously, or at least that's what many judges have reasoned. A still riper irony is that in aspiring to correct scientific and medical error everywhere else, courts have become steadily more willing to tolerate quackery on the witness stand (Huber 1991, 3).

A few years after the publication of Huber's book, the Supreme Court took a step in the direction he and other critics suggested. In *Daubert v. Merrell Dow Pharmaceuticals, Inc.* (1993),[6] the Court determined that the Federal Rules of Evidence mandated that expert testimony be subject to a reliability test and not, as had previously been the case, a "general acceptance test."[7] *Daubert* is a federal decision, but many state courts have adopted it as well. By mid-2003, twenty-seven states had adopted tests consistent with *Daubert* (Bernstein and Jackson 2004).

The Daubert decision and its progeny suggest a more fruitful way of looking at tort reform. Instead of thinking up new ways to constrain juries or pitting juries against judges, we need to think of ways to help juries arrive at better decisions. It's difficult enough for a lay jury to evaluate scientific information, but its job becomes well nigh impossible when lawyers are free to muddy the waters by introducing theories of dubious scientific merit. One way of reading *Daubert* is that it asks judges to filter the waters so that juries are presented with the best evidence, both pro and con, to evaluate the case at hand. The goal then is not to eliminate juries, but to help them to perform their task better.

Another simple reform along these lines cries out for implementation—jury note-taking. It's an amazing travesty that in many court systems today, juries are still not allowed to take notes! If one of us told our department chairperson that we had forbidden students to take notes on the theory that this is a better way of arriving at the truth, we would be laughed out of the office, if not brought up on charges of academic negligence. Yet, juries are not allowed pen and paper. Even pen and paper is outmoded—why should juries not be permitted to use laptops and PDAs, just like our students?

It's foolish to present juries with a blizzard of junk science, give them no tools to sift the wheat from the chaff, and then complain that juries do a poor job. We need to help juries to do their jobs. Judges must play a key role in this process.

LIMITATIONS ON JUDGES AND JURIES BY CONTRACT

A related way of easing the burden on judges and juries is to recognize that tort law is an essentially inferior, but sometimes necessary, alternative to market exchange via contract. Most goods can be easily bought and sold. If you have a car that I want to use, I can purchase that in a market exchange. Under ordinary circumstances, the courts do not try to allocate your car to its highest value use by specifying the conditions under which I have use rights, even absent purchase. We do not want the courts to attempt to make these allocations because it is clear that market exchange via contract is more efficient and quite likely more just. You and I are more likely to contract to a wealth-maximizing and mutually agreeable exchange than the court is likely to impose such an exchange because you and I have information—about our preferences, opportunities, and costs—that the courts cannot know. Furthermore, unlike the courts, you and I have strong incentives to use our knowledge and entrepreneurial skills to maximize the value of a market exchange.

If market exchange is superior to allocation by the courts, why use the courts at all? In fact, in a world of zero transactions costs, all goods and services, including legal rights, could be bought and sold in markets. For example, if I wanted to take some action, such as driving speedily, that raises your probability of harm, then I could purchase that right at a mutually agreed upon price. Thus, if transactions costs were low, markets would allocate legal rights as efficiently as they do other goods, and tort law would be moot (Krauss 1999). Transactions costs, however, can sometimes preclude efficient exchange—it's simply too expensive, for example, to use markets to contract in advance about auto accidents that may occur in the future between complete strangers.

Tort law is a useful supplement to market exchange, but it is not a good substitute.

Unfortunately, over the twentieth century and especially since the 1960s, tort law has been killing contract law (Gilmore 1974; Atiyah 1979; but see also Buckley 1999). The reason for this has not been increased transactions costs—one can hardly claim that the contracts that the courts were voiding could not have been formed because transactions costs were too high! Instead tort law has been substituted for contract law, even when the parties are in a contractual relationship—and sometimes even against the *ex-ante* wishes of the bargain makers.

Contracts can and should substitute for much of tort law. A doctor and her patient, for example, have ample opportunities to create a contract specifying how they would like to handle any injuries that may result from medical procedures. Such a contract can cover both procedural and substantive aspects of dispute resolution. For example, a patient and physician may agree that disputes will be decided by an independent panel of experts (equal numbers chosen by both sides for example), they might agree to refer the case to binding arbitration, or they might agree that the case will be heard in court, but that pain and suffering awards would be limited to $250,000.

It might be objected that such limitations are one-sided. On the contrary, there are sound reasons why both patient and physician can benefit from tort reform by contract (Rubin 1993). Moreover, many states have already capped noneconomic damages. Does it make sense to allow legislators to statutorily limit damages, but not allow individuals to do so by contract?

Similarly, warranties and waivers can be used to create a product-liability law based upon contract.

Although avenues for statutorily reforming the tort system exist, there is much to recommend letting individuals do it themselves. If contractual parties agree that the court system is ill-suited to deciding their dispute, either because judges and juries lack the incentives or the capacity to decide the case, the best time to opt out of the legal system is before a dispute arises.

Notes

CHAPTER I

1 Albeit the plaintiff lawyers were not as good as they thought, because the judge gave them less than half of what they asked for. See Brenda Sandburg. 2004. Judge Slashes Fees in Microsoft Class Action. The Recorder 09-14-2004. Available at http://www.law.com/jsp/article.jsp?id=1095107239344 (Last accessed July 10, 2005).

2 Even though most people have heard about the McDonald's coffee case, few know the actual facts. Mrs. Stella Liebeck, 79, was in the passenger seat of her grandson's car when she was severely burned by McDonald's coffee in 1992. During discovery McDonald's disclosed that it held its coffee at between 180 and 190 degrees Fahrenheit to maintain optimum taste. This is hotter than coffee served at home, which is usually between 135 to 140 degrees but a little bit below what many coffee experts consider to be the optimal temperature of 197 to 205 degrees (e.g. see Coffee FAQ at http://coffeefaq.com/coffaq1.htm).

  The jury awarded $200,000 in compensatory damages and $2.7 million in punitive damages. The jury reduced its own compensatory award to $160,000 because it found Liebeck 20 percent at fault. The trial court reduced the punitive award to $480,000. We do not know the ultimate payment in the case as the parties entered into a post-verdict settlement that was not disclosed publicly.

  Following the suit, a post-verdict investigation by a local newspaper found that the temperature of coffee at the local Albuquerque McDonald's had dropped to 158 degrees Fahrenheit. This annoys those of us who like to add cream to our coffee before drinking it but probably does result in fewer scaldings.

  See *Liebeck v. McDonald's Restaurants*, No. CV-93-02419, 1995 (N.M. Dist. Aug. 18, 1994).

3 Public Citizen's Response to Newsweek, available online at http://www.citizen.org/documents/Newsweek_Response.pdf, last accessed July 17, 2005.

4 We use the term tort expenditures rather than tort costs because the Tillinghast figures include transfers that directly induce no consumption of real resources. A

true measure of costs would exclude some of the Tillinghast figures but include others that they do not. Rather than focusing on the absolute level of expenditures we draw attention to the increase in expenditures as a fraction of GDP.

5 It is perhaps more accurate to say that these reforms were passed in the mid-1970s and early 1980s but in many cases, such as California, their implementation was delayed by court challenges often delaying implementation for a decade.

6 *Liebeck v. McDonald's Restaurants*, No. CV-93-02419, 1995 (N.M. Dist. Aug. 18, 1994).

7 Consider the case of black lung disease, or pneumoconiosis, that affected a large number of individuals working in mines. In 1977, Congress created the Black Lung Disability Trust Fund to compensate miners afflicted with black lung disease who had worked in mining prior to 1970. The basic logic of the Fund was that deterrence was not an issue as efforts were being made to prevent the illness and compensating victims no longer need to be handled through the court system. For an interesting discussion of the issue of asbestos, see Carrol et al. (2002).

8 There is, indeed, evidence that tort law causes safety improvements in driving. Starting in the 1970s, a number of states adopted no-fault auto insurance laws that remove or restrict the liability for auto accidents because a driver's own insurer pays their accident costs regardless of how the accident happened. The effect of this change is to shift some of the cost of auto-related injuries from potential defendants to potential plaintiffs. Theoretically a driver who knows he is potentially liable for the costs of an accident resulting from his negligence will take that fact into account in deciding how safely to drive. This weakening of torts deterrent effect is estimated to have caused a 10–15% increase in the highway fatality rate (Landes, 1982). The magnituded of this effect, however, has led some to question whether the impact is due to no-fault or trends in the data (see Loughran (2001).

CHAPTER 2

1 Morley Safer. Jackpot Justice. 60 Minutes, Nov. 24, 03.

2 Date is for 1999-2000, see U.S. Census Data for Jefferson County, MS available at http://www.fedstats.gov/qf/states/28/28063.html last accessed Jan. 31, 05.

3 The *60 Minutes* episode featured a plaintiff who had won millions in a lawsuit against the manufacturers of the diet drug Redux (his injuries had not dissuaded him about the benefits of weight-loss pharmaceuticals—he promptly started on Meridia only to sue the manufacturers of that drug). The plaintiff hinted that the jury had been in on the deal that awarded him his millions. This is not such a surprising claim given the size of the county and the number of lawsuits. In

another prominent case the mayor of Fayette (the county seat), the father of a constable, the wife of a local judge and the sister-in-law of the circuit clerk who helps select jurors were all plaintiffs (Pear 2001). Of course, after the segment appeared 60 Minutes was sued by several jurors from the case for over 6 *billion* dollars.

4 Daniels and Martin (1995) refer to "socioeconomic" factors to explain the variability in awards and win rates that they find across counties, but they do not attempt to test this hypothesis or further investigate which socioeconomic factors may or may not be important. A New York Commission also found perceptions "that awards given by juries to minority plaintiffs in civil cases vary in direct relation to the size of the minority population in the county where the litigation is brought, (Report of the New York State Judicial Commission on Minorities at 44)." The Commission, however, assumed that the result was due to bias against minority plaintiffs and did not investigate the possibility of a independent role for jury demographics.

In an experimental study, Kip Viscusi finds that blacks and Hispanics are less able or less willing to follow specific numerical instructions in assessing punitive damages (Viscusi 2001).

In a paper published after our paper was writen, Eisenberg and Wells (2002) find that awards tend to increase in poverty rates, but they do not find a racial effect similar to the one that we find. In part, this may be due to a different definition of poverty rates than the one used in this paper—we discuss this difference at greater length below.

5 Under some conditions, win rates tend towards 50% regardless of jury characteristics, this makes any relationship between win rates and jury demographics very difficult to identify. See further below and Priest and Klein (1984).

6 Like other studies, JVR bases most of its results on documents known as court reporters. A potential problem, however, is that JVR also surveys legal newspapers to collect information on cases that it might have missed in its survey of court reporters, and this collection strategy may bias attention towards large awards. (The use of legal newspaper reports is not unusual. Daniels and Martin (1985), Karpoff and Lott (1993, 1999) and Alexander, Arlen, and Cohen (1999) all use data either directly from newspapers or from Lexis/Nexis or court reporters which themselves draw from from legal newspapers.) Because our focus is the *change* in tort awards induced by a change in county demographics, oversampling of large awards does not present a problem. Indeed, to the extent that large awards are a subject of particular concern, any oversampling can be beneficial. Without qualification, however, the average awards in this study should not be taken to represent population averages.

7 The Federal Court data has been used in a number of papers by Clermont and Eisenberg and is described in greater detail in Clermont and Eisenberg (1992, 1998).

8 An earlier version of our paper aggregated on districts rather than divisions and the even smaller trial units. We are very grateful to Ted Eisenberg for sending us information and data on trial units. A detailed discussion of trial units and how they can be connected to the Federal data can be found in Eisenberg and Wells (2002).

9 The Federal data set has one other limitation: It has top and bottom limits. The top limit is at $9,999,000—that is, all awards larger than this figure are coded at $9,999,000. Awards smaller than $1000 are coded at zero. The bottom limit is likely to be innocuous, however, because the maximum error introduced by bottom-coding is $999 while the maximum error induced by top-limit could easily run into the millions of dollars (some 2.5% of awards in our sample are top-limited.) We will use an interval/censored regression procedure to control for top and bottom limits in the Federal data.

10 The Jury Selection and Service Act of 1968 (JSSA) was passed to ensure that Federal juries be randomly drawn from a "fair cross-section" of the relevant jury pool. Most states have similar laws. The Supreme Court held that race-based peremptory challenges by either the plaintiff or defendant violate the equal protection rights of the challenged jurors (*Edmonson v. Leesville Concrete Co*, 111 S. Ct. 2077 (1991)) On peremptory challenges in criminal and civil trials see Raeber (1992).

It is not necessary for our results (nor do we claim) that minority underrepresentation has been eliminated. On the issue of underrepresentation see Bueker (1997) and Seltzer, Copacino and Donahoe (1996).

11 An alternative concern is that economic excuses from jury duty would tend to make minority and low-income jurors more common than the county demographic data would suggest. We are less concerned with this than with potential efforts to exclude minorities as this would tend to bias our results toward zero. However, several studies have examined the role of economic excuses and overall the results suggest that excuses do not systematically alter the jury pool (Cecil, Lind and Bermant 1987).

12 The poverty rate is defined as the number of persons in poverty in the county identified by the 1990 census divided by the county population in 1990.

13 Following the suggestion of a referee, we also restricted the State Court data to make the case types even more similar to those in the JVR dataset—primarily by removing contract, libel and real property cases. The restriction leaves us with 2,272 observations. The results, however, are virtually identical—the coefficient on poverty in the restricted regression is 33,249.

14 Note that to control for heteroscedasticity we use heteroscedastic-consistent errors throughout our regressions and we control for top and bottom coding using an interval/censored regression procedure in the Federal data.

15 The regressions in Table 4 contains only county level variables (or trial unit level variables in the case of the Federal data); the true number of observations (coun-

ties=1803) is therefore less than the number of award observations (41,150) and the standard errors in Table 3 are inflated. Running the same regression (JVR data) with the average county award as the independent variable, however, leads to very similar results. The reason for presenting the awards regression rather than the county regression is that we shortly introduce case-level variables into the analysis and the presentation facilitates comparisons.

16 To calculate these probabilities, we plotted a kernel density estimate (essentially a sophisticated histogram) of the logged award distribution for low (0–5%), medium (20–25%) and high (35%+) poverty counties. See Helland and Tabarrok (2003) for more details.

17 Age 15-plus and age 20-plus population figures have a correlation of .933 so the age 20-plus population will be an extremely good proxy for the age 18-plus population. To the extent that 18–19 year olds are less likely to serve on juries than those of greater age the age 20-plus figures are superior.

18 In their regression, Eisenberg and Wells (2002) use the standard definition of the black and Hispanic poverty rates, rather than our definition that focuses on jury composition. Eisenberg and Wells, therefore, are testing different but complementary hypotheses to the ones that we test. Eisenberg and Wells find that average county awards are not greatly affected by the percentage of blacks or Hispanics in poverty. This result gives credence to our jury-composition theory because it tells us that what is driving the result is not a factor associated with high black or Hispanic poverty. Rather, it is the number of blacks and Hispanics in poverty relative to the county population that matters not the number of blacks or Hispanic in poverty relative to the total county population of blacks and Hispanics.

19 We have also run this specification using county means. Noting that all variables in the following denote county means and standard errors are in parentheses the regressions results are taward = 202,706 (26,552) – 4,293 × WPOV (1,247) + 21,373 × BPOV (4609) + 66,531 × HPOV (11,626). The regression is weighted to produce robust standard errors. Note that all results are statistically significant at the greater than 1% level.

20 We have also experimented with including a dummy variable whenever a county contained an MSA or part of an MSA. An MSA dummy was never statistically significant.

21 Note that we do not log the poverty rates—thus we have a semi-log functional form which implies that the beta coefficients can be understood as giving the percentage effect on awards of a unit increase in poverty rates.

22 In the State Court data a number of states are represented by only one county (these are GA, HI, IN, KY, MN, MO, NY, VA, WA, WI). Since there is no in-state variation in poverty rates in these states, data from these states does not contribute directly to the measurement of the poverty coefficients. The information in these states does, however, help to compute the coefficients on the

variables that differ across cases (the injury and case type variables). Better information on the impact of the case variables will improve the estimates of the poverty coefficients thus information from these states contributes indirectly to the measurement of interest. Dropping these states altogether leads to similar coefficients (–15,000, 71,860, and –103,600) on the coefficients for white, black and Hispanic poverty respectively.

23 In addition, in the state court data set in particular the variation in the Hispanic poverty rate is quite low (the maximum range is 0–8% in the state court data, compared to 0–30% in the JVR data and 0–37% in the Federal data).

24 Note that the state court data is a random sample from only one month. The actual overlap of cases between the restricted JVR and state court data set, therefore, is likely to be zero or negligible.

25 Ideally, we would like to perform a similar estimate for the State Court and Federal data sets. However, in both of these cases, the cell sizes are too small for medical-malpractice or product-liability cases to permit meaningful analysis.

26 At the suggestion of a referee we also ran separate regressions just on product-liability and medical-malpractice cases respectively. In both cases, the results were similar (although somewhat larger) than the effects we report. Results are available upon request.

27 In regressions not reported we found no evidence for a nonlinear effect in white poverty rates.

28 Trials are the most important output of the civil justice system in the sense that trials are the final output without which no other output is possible.

29 We use a Probit regression.

30 In the standard model, the savings from settling rather than trying a case are assumed to be a constant fraction of the potential judgment (e.g. see Priest and Klein (1984) and Waldfogel (1995), setting $(C–S)/J = c$.) With this assumption there is no selection on awards. Selection on awards can never be strong because if high-award cases rarely go to trial their outcome becomes more uncertain, which increases the number of these cases that will fail to settle.

CHAPTER 3

1 Reported in United States General Accounting Office (U.S. GAO), *Report to Congressional Requesters, Medical Malpractice: Case Study in North Carolina* (Dec, 1986). This and many other similar quotations can also be found in Vidmar (1997), see also Adler (1994).

2 Schuck (1993) reviews a number of jury reform proposals. Bernstein (1996) is particularly antagonistic towards juries.

3 See, for example, Izard (1998), or Haydock and Sonsteng (1991).

4 Interestingly, this rate of agreement is almost identical to the appeals courts affirmation rate of trial verdicts (81 percent). See Clermont and Eisenberg (1999).

5 The Kalven and Zeisel results are supported by other research showing that judges and juries reach similar decisions in similar cases and that juries appear to respond to information in reasonable ways. A number of papers in Litan (1993) make this point, see especially Lempert (1993:235) who writes "The weight of evidence indicates that juries can reach rationally defensible verdicts in complex cases [and] that we cannot assume that judges in complex cases will perform better than juries..." The literature on the quality of jury decision-making is reviewed in Hans and Vidmar (1986), see also Clermont and Eisenberg (1992).

6 The graph is estimated using a kernel density to produce what can be thought of as a smoothed histogram. We use a bi-weight kernel with smoothing parameter optimized on the assumption that the underlying data is normally distributed (see Silverman (1986) for more information on kernel estimation.) The use of other kernels and/or smoothing parameters does not materially affect the results.

7 Tabarrok and Helland (1999) and Helland and Tabarrok (2002) show that awards are higher in product-liability and medical-malpractice cases than in other cases even after controlling for injuries.

8 We use log awards so that a handful of very large awards will not bias the results.

9 Further below we also report what judges would have done had they decided the cases that actually went to juries.

10 Under the null hypothesis we initially expect judge and jury awards to be the same. The "unexplained" difference is thus 100 percent–31 percent=69 percent. If we can explain 100-x of this difference then the ratio of the unexplained to the explained is (100–x)/(100–31). Note that when x=31, 100 percent of the difference is explained and when x=100, as would have been the case if the sample of cases types going to judge and jury trial were the same, then none of the difference is explained. Letting x be 63 we have that 53 percent of the difference in averages is explained by differences in case types.

11 To prevent perfect collinearity with the intercept term we suppress Wrongful Termination.

12 No state prohibits punitive damages absolutely. Punitive damages are prohibited in New Hampshire, for example, except where explicitly allowed for by statute.

13 The American Tort Reform Association (ATRA) home page, http://www.atra .org/, contains information on tort reform legislation by state.

14 Some of these results may be subject to endogeneity problems—perhaps states with above average punitive damage awards are more likely to pass evidence standards than other states—so we cannot make definitive conclusions about the effect of various laws. "Reduced form estimates," however, are all we need in order to examine the role of sample effects in explaining differences in average judge and jury awards.

15 There are no class-action suits in our sample.

16 We also included a specification with poverty and poverty squared. The high correlation of these variables made interpretation more difficult than with the simpler specification used in the text, but the comparison across judge and juries was similar.

17 The case category variables explain a larger fraction of the judge/jury difference than the "injury" set of variables regardless of the order in which variables are added. Since the marginal explanatory power does vary, however, with the order in which variables are added, the total explanatory power is the more important result.

CHAPTER 4

1 Many judges in appointed states maintain their office by running in a retention election. These elections are *unopposed* elections in which the judge is either voted up or down. Hall and Aspin (1987) find that retention elections return the incumbent to office 98.8% of the time. Carbon (1980) points out that retention elections were designed to create lengthy judicial tenures and to insulate judges from the public. Retention elections also insulate appointed judges from pressures from the governor. Since retention elections are essentially perfunctory, we define states using initial appointment followed by retention elections as appointed states.

2 The states with partisan elections are Alabama, Arkansas, Illinois, Mississippi, New York, North Carolina, Pennsylvania, Tennessee, Texas, and West Virginia. For more details on our classification of electoral systems see the *Book of the States* and the discussion in Tabarrok and Helland (1999). Our conclusions are robust to reclassification of any states with significant mixing of elected and nonelected elements (eg. NY has a mixed system).

3 The discovery that sociological characteristics do not differ across selection mechanisms strengthens our conclusion that the primary independent variable is the incentive structure. Ashenfelter, Eisenberg, and Schwab (1995) find that sociological characteristics of judges are of no help in predicting outcomes.

4 Tabarrok and Helland (1999) do not control for selection effects. The data set used in this chapter is deeper as well as longer than that used in our earlier paper. In our earlier paper, control variables such as poverty rates were measured at the state level. In this paper, all of our control variables are case specific or measured at the level of the county in which the trial takes place.

5 Clermont and Eisenberg (1996) examine whether the federal courts are biased against foreign corporations.

6 Judges may understand the negative impact that excessively generous trial awards can have on insurance costs, wages and employment, and economic growth.

Nevertheless, state judges have little to gain from more restrained interpretations of liability law. A judgment in favor of a defendant enriches an out-of-state corporation but has little effect on national employment and even less effect on in-state employment or wages. The gains from restrained interpretation of liability laws are external to the state judges who interpret those laws. But the benefits of liberal judgments, in votes and campaign contributions according to Neely's hypothesis, accrue directly. Similarly, voters have few incentives to demand changes in liability law that primarily benefit out-of-state corporations. The median voter, therefore, is likely to support judges who redistribute income to in-state plaintiffs.

7 Other observers have also noted that elected judges are easier to influence than appointed judges. Herman Wrice, the founder of an anti-drug citizen's group in the Mantua section of Philadelphia, notes that "In a city where judges are elected, a few members of Mantua Against Drugs assembled in the court room can add thousands of dollars to the price of bail." Quoted in Benson (1998, 124).

8 We removed all class-action suits from our sample both because it is difficult to code for injuries in these cases and because plaintiffs in these suits may come from many states.

9 No state prohibits punitive damages absolutely and completely. Punitive damages are prohibited in New Hampshire, for example, except where explicitly allowed for by statute.

10 Percentage changes may be calculated taking the inverse log, subtracting 1 and multiplying by 100, e.g. $(e^{.45591*Ln(40)} - 1) \times 100 = 437$.

11 Calculated from $(e^{1.0286} - 1) \times 100$.

12 The F test for the restriction Partisan Out = NonPartisan Out is $F[1,29209] = 10.5046$ with $p = 0.0014$.

13 We cannot reject the hypothesis that NonPartisan Out = NonPartisan In, $F[1,29209] = 0.0191$ with $p = .8605$. The restriction Partisan Out = Partisan In has $F[1,29209] = 4.2963$ with $p = 0.0360$.

14 The restriction (Partisan Out – Partisan In) – (NonPartisan Out – NonPartisan In) has $F[1,29209] = 3.1432$ with $p = 0.0725$. The restriction Partisan In = NonPartisan In has $F[1,29209] = 10.9615$ with $p = 0.011$.

15 The state-level fixed effects made it very difficult to compute the heteroscedastic consistent var-covariance matrix so we relied for this F-test only on OLS standard errors.

16 The definitive source for diversity of citizenship law is Wright (1994). Posner (1996) and Lieberman (1992) give short overviews.

17 Results from the federal and state settlement and win equations are available from the authors upon request.

18 We use the location of the federal court to deduce the state law which the court is using to decide the case. It is possible that a case adjudicated in a federal court in state A is decided based upon the law of state B. In our sample of cases, which are

personal-injury cases in which an individual sues a corporation, this is unlikely to occur. In over 99% of these types of cases the plaintiff (an individual) resides in the state in which the trial takes place. Furthermore, the traditional common law rule is that the law of the state where the injury occurred is the law to be applied. Since the vast majority of personal injuries occur in the state in which the plaintiff resides, the traditional rule strongly suggests that the law of the state in which the trial takes places is the ruling law. In some states, the courts analyze the respective interests of the states to decide the law to be applied. Prime among the determinants a court will use to deduce a state's "interests", however, is the place of the injury (and also the residence of the parties to the dispute). For more details see Posner (1998) and the Restatement (Second) of Conflict of Laws.

CHAPTER 5

1 U.S. Department of Health and Human Services, *Confronting the New Health Care Crisis: Improving Health Care Quality and Lowering Costs by Fixing Our Medical Liability System* (Washington, D.C., 24 July 2002), 2, 3, 12, 13, http://aspe.hhs.gov/daltcp/reports/litrefm.pdf (accessed March 22, 2005).

2 Perhaps due to the uproar over the first announcement, the Attorneys General, the tobacco companies, and the lawyers have kept the exact fees secret (Viscusi 2002: 4). Robert Levy calculates that the fee in the Florida, Mississippi, Texas case was equivalent to over $14,000 dollars an hour, assuming 12 hours of work a day, 7 days a week for 42 months (Levy 1999: 27). See, also, Brickman (2003: 653, 660 n.13). Brickman cites equivalent hourly fees in the hundreds of thousands of dollars an hour once hours are estimated realistically.

3 *Intermediate Sanctions Compensatory Revenue Adjustment Act of 2003*, 108th Cong., 1st sess., S. 887.

4 See, for example, *Public Citizen Litigation Group Quarterly Update*, July 28, 2000, http://www.citizen.org/litigation/about/articles.cfm?ID=554; last accessed June 20, 2005. Walter E. Dellinger, III, Testimony before the Senate Committee on the Judiciary, *Class Action Litigation*, 107th Cong., 2d sess.,July 31, 2002.

5 FTC, "Announced Actions for June 6, 2003," *Press Release*, 6 June 2003, http://www.ftc.gov/opa/2003/06/fyi0336.htm (accessed April 25, 2005); FTC, "Announced Actions for March 17, 2004," *Press Release*, http://www.ftc.gov/opa/2004/03/fyi0419.htm (accessed April, 25 2005); *Class Action Fairness Act of 2005*, Public Law 109–2, 109th Cong., 1st sess. (18 February 2005).

6 Theoretically, tort law can be understood as an attempt to mimic contractual considerations: What arrangements would the parties have agreed to if they had been able to contract? (Rubin 1993) Unlike contract law, however, where judges and juries can ground their decisions in actual contracts, tort disputes arise pre-

cisely when parties interact without contract. Without the grounding in practice, the decisions of judges and juries may generate inefficiencies.

7 It is slightly puzzling, however, that contingency fees are virtually unheard of
in non-US legal systems. Perhaps this has to do with cultural idiosyncracies,
such as the more entrepreneur friendly climate in the U.S., as opposed to any
particular beliefs about the effects of contingency fees. Analagously, Robert
Gordon points out that the use of venture capital is far more widespread in the
U.S. than it is in the rest of the world. (See Robert Gordon, "Why Was Europe
Left at the Station When America's Productivity Locomotive Departed?" *NBER
Working Paper* 10661. (2004)) Another potential puzzle arises regarding the fact
that contingency fees are generally barred in criminal law cases and family law
cases. Perhaps these restrictions stem from valuation problems (e.g., how can an
acquittal be valued in a reasonable way to generate a basis on which to apply the
contingency fee). Research on these questions would be very valuable.

8 For an analysis see Emons and Garoupa (2004). For more on contingent fees as
a device to increase effort see Schwartz and Mitchell (1970: 1125–62); Danzon
(1983: 213–24); and Hay (1996:503–33). In *Kritzer* (2002: 739–784), Kritzer argues that contingency fees are common in other countries but on close inspection
many of these are conditional rather than contingent fees.

9 See Rubinfeld and Scotchmer (1993). The signaling model can be modified in a
variety of ways. Instead of the signal being sent by the lawyer, for example, one
can model a situation where clients use the contingent fee to signal the strength
of their case. Other variants are also possible. Papers in the signaling literature
include Smith and Cox (1958); Dana and Spier (1993); and Rickman (1999). For a
good survey of these and other issues see Rubinfeld and Scotchmer (1998).

10 For a good argument along these lines see Hyman and Silver (2001).

11 Robin Hanson provides a strong argument for the value of compensating doctors
on a contingent basis. One potentially relevant difference between medicine and
law is the widespread use of health insurance (especially managed care systems)
which dampens some of the benefits of a contingent fee system. Perhaps in a fee
for service health system, we might observe more contingent fees for doctors.
(Hanson 1994: 135–141).

12 Judge Richard Posner used this argument in several dissents from decisions ap-
pointing counsel for prisoners in civil rights suits. See *McKeever v. Israel*, 689
F.2d 1315, 1324–1325 (7th Cir. 1982) and *Merritt v. Faulkner*, 697 F. 2d 761, 769–
770 (7th Cir. 1983).

13 See http://www.lawcash.net/about/about.html (accessed March 23, 2005). Conditional loans are also called non-recourse loans. See also http://www.expertlaw.
com/library/pubarticles/lawsuit_funding.html for more on non-recourse loans
(accessed March 23, 2005).

14 The survey is available from the Inter-University Consortium for Political and
Social Research (ICPSR 6587) at http://www.icpsr.umich.edu/. It covers tort,

contract and real property cases disposed of between July 1, 1991 and June 30, 1992 in 45 jurisdictions chosen to represent the 75 most populous counties in the nation (these counties account for about half of all civil filings.) A more complete description of the dataset and our empirical technique can be found in Helland and Tabarrok (2003).

15 Further details on tests can be found in Helland and Tabarrok (2003).

16 Miller (1987: 199). The basic result, however, can be reversed with minor changes in assumptions. For one example, Polinksy and Rubinfeld (2002: 217–225).

17 For an example of this fee arrangement using third-party financing see Polinksy and Rubinfeld (2002).

18 Recent work by Helland and Klick (2005) suggests that judges prove to be ineffective protectors of the plaintiff class, placing their own desire to clear the court's docket of the case before the interests of the nominal plaintiffs.

19 Tillinghast-Towers Perrin. U.S. Tort Costs: 2000 Update. Trends and Findings on the Costs of the U.S. Tort System. 2000.

20 Harvard Medical Practice Study, "Patients, Doctors, and Lawyers: Medical Injury, Malpractice Litigation, and Patient Compensation in New York," a report of the Harvard Medical Practice Study to the State of New York (Cambridge: Ma: The President and Fellows of Harvard College).

CHAPTER 6

1 From Douglas, Linder. 2001. The Zenger Trial: An Account. Available at http://www.law.umkc.edu/faculty/projects/ftrials/zenger/zenger.html. Last accessed June 1, 05. See also Putnam (1997).

2 No. 00-L-525 (Ill. Cir. Ct. Madison County filed June 13, 2000). See Beisner and Miller (2001) for this case and others.

3 746 N.E. 2d 1242 (Ill. Ct. App. 2001).

4 The key statute is 28 U.S.C. Section 1332. For court interpretation see *Strawbridge v. Curtiss*, 7 U.S. (3 Cranch) 267 (1806). Note that the legislation and its interpretation long predate modern class action law.

5 Class Action Fairness Act of 2000, S. Rep. No. 106-420, 106th Congress (2000) at 20. Quoted in Beisner and Miller (2001).

6 509 U.S. 579 (1993)

7 The Daubert case was followed up by *General Electric Co. v. Joiner* (1997), which made clear that judges should examine both a witness's methodology and the link between the evidence that the expert offered and the conclusions drawn by the witness. Then *Kumho Tire Co. v. Carmichael* (1999)extended the Daubert-sanctioned gatekeeping role from scientific evidence to all expert testimony. The three cases together are known as the Daubert trilogy.

References

Abraham, Kenneth and Lance Liebman. "Private Insurance, Social Insurance, and Tort Reform: Toward a New Vision of Compensation for Illness and Injury." *Columbia Law Review* 93 (1993); 75–118.

Aczel, Amir. *Complete Business Statistics, 3rd ed.* Homewood, IL: Richard Irwin, 1996.

Adler, Stephen J. *The Jury: Trial and Error in the American Courtroom.* Random House, 1994.

Alexander, C. R., J. Arlen, and M. A. Cohen. "Regulating Corporate Criminal Sanctions: Federal Guidelines and the Sentencing of Public Firms." *Journal of Law and Economics* 42 (1) (1999): 393–422.

Alozie, N. O. "Distribution of Women and Minority Judges: The Effects of Judicial Selection Methods." *Social Science Quarterly* 71(2) (1990): 315–326.

American Medical Association. *AMA Tort Reform Compendium.* Chicago: American Medical Association, 1989.

Atiyah, P. S. *The Rise and Fall of Freedom of Contract.* Oxford: Oxford University Press, 1979.

Baum, L. "Electing Judges." In *Contemplating Courts*, ed. L. Epstein. Washington, D.C.: CQ Press, 1995, 18–43.

Baumol, William. "Entrepreneurship: Productive, Unproductive and Destructive." *Journal of Political Economy* 98(5) (1990): 915.

Beisner, John and Jessica Davidson Miller. "They're Making a Federal Case Out of It... In State Court." *Harvard Journal of Law and Public Policy* 25(1) (2001): 143–207.

Benson, Bruce L. *To Serve and Protect: Privatization and Community in Criminal Justice.* New York: New York University Press for the Independent Institute, 1998.

Bernard, J. L. "Between the Race of the Defendant and That of Jurors in Determining Verdicts." *Law & Psychology Review* 5 (1979): 103–111.

Bernstein, D. E. "Procedural Tort Reform: Lessons from Other Nations," *Regulation* 19(1): (1996), http://www.cato.org/pubs/regulation/reg19n1e.html, (accessed April 25, 2005).

Born, Patricia H. and W. Kip Viscusi. "The Distribution of the Insurance Market Effects of Tort Liability Reforms." *Brookings Papers on Economic Activity* (1998): 55–100.

Boyes, W. J., D. L. Hoffman, and S. A. Low. "An Econometric Analysis of the Bank Credit Scoring Problem." *Journal of Econometrics* 40 (1989): 3–14.

Bradford, Laura. 2003. "Fat Foods: Back in Court." *Time,* August, 03, 2003. http://www.time.com/time/insidebiz/article/0,9171,1101030811-472858,00.html.

Brickman, Lester. "Effective Hourly Rates of Contingency Fee Lawyers: Competing Data and Non-Competitive Fees." *Washington Law Quarterly* 81(3) (2003).

———. "The Market for Contingent Fee-Financed Tort Litigation: Is It Price Competitive?" *Cardozo Law Review* 25 (2003): 65–128.

———. "On the Theory Class's Theories of Asbestos Litigation: The Disconnect Between Scholarship and Reality." *Pepperdine Law Review* 31(33) (2004): 33–170.

Buckley, F. H. *The Fall and Rise of Freedom of Contract.* Duke University Press, 1999.

Bueker, J. P. "Jury Source Lists: Does Supplementation Really Work?" *Cornell Law Review* 82 (1997): 390–431.

Bureau of Economic Analysis. "Personal Consumption Expenditures—New Autos." 2004.

California Civil Code. "Deering's California Codes Annotated," in I. Matthew Bender & Co., 2003.

Campbell, Thomas J., Daniel P. Kessler, and George B. Shepherd."The Link between Liability Reforms and Productivity: Some Empirical Evidence." *Brookings Papers on Economic Activity 1998* (1999): 107–137.

Carbon, S. B. "Judicial Retention Elections: Are They Serving Their Intended Purpose?" *Judicature* 64(5) (1980): 211–233.

Cecil, J. S., A. E. Lind, and G. Bermant. *Jury Service in Lengthy Civil Trials.* Washington, D.C.: The Federal Judicial Center, 1987.

Chin, A. and M. A. Peterson. *Deep Pockets, Empty Pockets: Who Wins in Cook County Jury Trials.* Santa Monica, Calif.: Rand Corp., 1985.

Clermont, Kevin M. and Theodore Eisenberg. "Appeal from Jury or Judge Trial: Defendants' Advantage" (lecture, the American Law and Economics Association annual meeting, 1999.

———. "Xenophilia in American Courts." *Harvard Law Review* 109(5) 1996: 1120–1143.

———. "Trial by Jury or Judge: Transcending Empiricism." *Cornell Law Review* 77 (1992): 1124–1177.

———. "Do Case Outcomes Really Reveal Anything About the Legal System? Win Rates and Removal Jurisdiction." *Cornell Law Review* 83 (1998): 581–607.

Congressional Budget Office. *The Economics of U.S. Tort Liability: A Primer.* Washington, D.C.: Congressional Budget Office, 2003.

Cooter, Robert D. and D. L. Rubinfeld. "Economic Analysis of Legal Disputes and Their Resolution." *Journal of Economic Literature* 27 (1989): 1067–1097.

Cooter, Robert D. and Thomas Ulen. *Law & Economics*. Reading, MA.: Addison-Wesley, 2000.

Craig, Andrew. "Product Liability and Safety in General Aviation." *The Liability Maze: The Impact of Liability Law on Safety and Innovation*. Washington, D.C.: Brookings Institution 1991.

Cumming, Douglas. "Settlement Disputes: Evidence From a Legal Practice Perspective." *European Journal of Law and Economics* 11(3) (2001): 249–280.

Cummins, J. David, Richard D. Phillips, and Mary A. Weiss. "The Incentive Effects of No-Fault Automobile Insurance." *Journal of Law and Economics* 44(2) (2001): 427–464.

Dana, James D. and Kathryn E. Spier. "Expertise and Contingency Fees: The Role of Asymmetric Information in Attorney Compensation." *Journal of Law, Economics & Organization* 9 (1993): 349–367.

Daniels, S. and J. Martin. *Civil Juries and the Politics of Reform*. Evanston, IL.: Northwestern University Press, 1995.

Danzon, Patricia M. "Contingency Fees for Personal Injury Litigation." *Bell Journal of Economics* 14 (1983): 213–224.

———. "Tort Reform: The Case of Medical Malpractice." *Oxford Review of Economic Policy* 10(1) (1994): 84–98.

Danzon, Patricia M. and L. A. Lillard. *The Resolution of Medical Malpractice Claims: Modelling the Bargaining Process*. Santa Monica, Calif.: Institute for Civil Justice (RAND Corporation), 1982. [R-2792-ICJ.]

———. "Settlement Out of Court: The Disposition of Medical Malpractice Claims." *Journal of Legal Studies* 12 (1983): 345–377.

Dellinger, III, Walter E. Testimony before the Senate Committee on the Judiciary, *Class Action Litigation*, 107th Cong., 2d sess., July 31, 2002.

Demsetz, Harold. "Information and Efficiency: Another Viewpoint." *Journal of Law and Economics* 12(1) (1969): 1.

Dewees, Donald, David Duff, and Michael Trebilcock. *Exploring the Domain of Accident Law: Taking the Facts Seriously*. New York: Oxford University Press, 1996.

Diamond, S. S. "Order in the Court: Consistency in Criminal Court Decisions." In *The Master Lecture Series: Psychology and the Law*, 123–146, edited by C. J. Scheirer and B. L. Hammonds, Vol. 2. Washington, D.C.: American Psychological Association, 1983.

Donohue III, J. J. "The Effect of Joint and Several Liability on Settlement: Comment on Kornhauser and Revesz." *Journal of Legal Studies* 27(1:2) (1994): 517–558.

Dubay, Lisa, Robert Kaestner, and Timothy Waidmann. "The Impact of Malpractice Fears on Cesarean Section Rates." *Journal of Health Economics* 18(4) (1999): 491–522.

———. "Medical Malpractice Liability and Its Effect on Prenatal Care Utilization and Infant Health." *Journal of Health Economics* 20(4) (2001) 591–611.

Dubois, P. "The Politics of Innovation in State Courts: The Merit Plan of Judicial Selection." *Publius* 20 (1990): 23–42.

Easterbrook, Frank. "The Limits of Antitrust." *Texas Law Review* 63 (1984): 1, 9–10.

Eisenberg, T. and M. T. Wells. "Trial Outcomes and Demographics: Is There a Bronx Effect?" *Texas Law Review* 80 (2002): 1839–1874.

Emons, Winand and Nuno M. Garoupa. "The Economics of US-Style Contingent Fees and UK-Style Conditional Fees," *CEPR Discussion Paper No. 4473*, July 23, 2004, http://www.cepr.org/pubs/dps/DP4473.asp (accessed April 27, 05).

Epstein, Richard A. *Modern Product Liability.* Westport, Conn.: Quorum Books, 1980.

———. *Simple Rules for a Complex World*. Boston: Harvard University Press, 1995.

Etzioni, A. "Inventing Hispanics: A Diverse Minority Resists Being Labeled." *Brookings Review* 20(1) (2002): 10–13.

Federal Trade Commission. "Announced Actions for June 6, 2003," *Press Release*, June 6, 2003, http://www.ftc.gov/opa/2003/06/fyi0336.htm (accessed April 25, 2005).

———. "Announced Actions for March 17, 2004," *Press Release*, March 17, 2005, http://www.ftc.gov/opa/2004/03/fyi0419.htm (accessed April, 25 2005).

Flango, V. and C. Ducat. "What Difference Does Method of Judicial Selection Make?" *The Justice System Journal* 5(1) (1979): 25–44.

Frankel, Alison. "Still Ticking." *American Lawyer*. March. 2005.

Friendly, Henry J. "The Historic Basis of Diversity Jurisdiction." *Harvard Law Review* 41 (1928): 483–510.

Gilmore, Grant. *The Death of Contract.* Columbus: Ohio State University Press, 1974.

Glick, H. P. *Courts, Politics, and Justice.* New York: McGraw-Hill Book Co., 1983.

Glick, H. P. and C. Emmert. "Selection Systems and Judicial Characteristics." *Judicature* 70 (1987): 228–235.

Glendon, Mary Ann. *A Nation Under Lawyers.* New York: Farrar, Straus and Giroux, 1994.

Goldman, L. "Toward a Colorblind Jury Selection Process: Applying the 'Batson Function' to Peremptory Challenges in Civil Litigation: Practice, Procedure and Review." *Texas Technology Law Review* 19 (1990): 921–.

Gordon, Robert. "Why Was Europe Left at the Station When America's Productivity Locomotive Departed?" (Working Paper 10661, *NBER*, 2004).

Gould, J. P. "The Economics of Legal Conflicts." *Journal of Legal Studies* 2 (1973): 279–300.

Grisham, John. *The King of Torts.* New York: Doubleday Books, 2003.

Greene, W. H. *Econometric Analysis.* 3rd ed. New York: Prentice Hall, 1997.

Hall, W. K. and L. T. Aspin. "What Twenty Years of Judicial Retention Elections Have Told Us." *Judicature* 70(6) (1987): 340–347.

Hans, V. P. and N. Vidmar. *Judging the Jury.* New York: Plenum Press, 1986.

Hanson, Robin. "Buy Health, Not Health Care." *Cato Journal* 14(1) (1994): 135–141.

Harvard Medical Practice Study. "Patients, Doctors, and Lawyers: Medical Injury, Malpractice Litigation, and Patient Compensation in New York." Cambridge, Mass.: The President and Fellows of Harvard College, 1994.

Hay, Bruce L. "Contingency Fees and Agency Costs." *Journal of Legal Studies* 23 (1996): 503–533.

Haydock, R. and J. Sonsteng. *Trial: Theories, Tactics, Techniques* (American Casebook Series). St. Paul, Minn.: West, 1991.

Hanssen, A. "The Effect of Judicial Institutions on Uncertainty and the Rate of Litigation: The Election Versus the Appointment of State Judges." *Journal of Legal Studies* 28(1) (1999): 205–232.

Heckman, J. "Sample Selection Bias as a Specification Error." *Econometrica* 47 (1979): 153–161.

Helland, Eric, Jonathan Klick, and Alexander Tabarrok. "Data Watch: Tort-Uring the Data." *Journal of Economic Perspectives* 19 (2005).

Helland, Eric and Alexander Tabarrok. "Contingency Fees, Settlement Delay, and Low-Quality Litigation: Empirical Evidence from Two Datasets." *Journal of Law, Economics & Organization* 19 (2003): 517–542.

———. "The Effect of Electoral Institutions on Tort Awards." *American Law and Economics Review* 4(2) (2002): 341–70. Originally written as a working paper, 1999.

———. 2003. Race, Poverty, and American Tort Awards: Evidence from Three Datasets. *Journal of Legal Studies* 32: 27–58.

———. "Runaway Judges? Selection Effects and the Jury," *Journal of Law, Economics and Organization* 16 (2) (2000): 306–333.

Hensler, Deborah R. "Revisiting the Monster: New Myths and Realities of Class Action and Other Large Scale Litigation." *Duke Journal of Comparative and International Law* 11(2) (2001): 179–214.

Hensler, Deborah R., Bonnie Dombey-Moore, Beth Giddens, Jennifer Gross, Erik Moller, and Nicholas Pace. *Class Action Dilemmas : Pursuing Public Goals for Private Gain*. Santa Monica, Calif.: Institute for Civil Justice (RAND Corp.), 1999a.

———. *Class Action Dilemmas: Pursuing Public Goals for Private Gain, Executive Summary*. Santa Monica, Calif.: Institute for Civil Justice (RAND Corp.), 1999b.

Hensler, Deborah R. and Thomas D Rowe Jr. "Beyond 'It Just Ain't Worth It': Alternative Strategies for Damage Class Action Reform." *Law and Contemporary Problems* 64(2–3), (2001): 137–61.

———. "Revisiting the Monster: New Myths and Realities of Class Action and Other Large Scale Litigation." *Duke Journal of Comparative and International Law* 11(2): 2001.

Hollandsworth, Skip. "The Lawsuit from Hell." *Texas Monthly.* June 1996.

Huber, Peter W. and Robert E. Litan, eds. *The Liability Maze: The Impact of Liability Law on Safety and Innovation*. Washington, D.C.: Brookings Institution, 1991.

Hughes, James W. and Edward A. Snyder. "Litigation and Settlement under the English and American Rules: Theory and Evidence." *Journal of Law and Economics* 38(1) (1995): 225–50.

Hyman, David A. and Charles Silver. "You Get What You Pay For: Results Based Compensation for Medical Care." *Washington and Lee Law Review* 58 (2001): 1427–90.

Izard, R. A. *Lawyers and Lawsuits: A Guide to Litigation.* New York: MacMillan Spectrum, 1998.

Jarrell, Gregg and Sam Peltzman. "The Impact of Product Recalls on the Wealth of Sellers." *Journal of Political Economy* 93(3) (1985): 512–36.

Johnson, S. L. "Black Innocence and the White Jury." *Michigan Law Review* 83 (1985): 1611–1708.

Kalven, Harry Jr. and Hans Zeisel. *The American Jury.* Boston: Little, Brown, 1966.

Karpoff, J. M. and J. R. J. Lott. "The Reputational Penalty Firms Bear from Committing Criminal Fraud." *Journal of Law and Economics* 36(2) (1993): 757–802.

———. "On the Determinants and Importance of Punitive Awards." *Journal of Law and Economics* 42(1) (1999): 527–73.

Kessler, Daniel and Mark McClellan. "Do Doctors Practice Defensive Medicine?" *Quarterly Journal of Economics* 111(2) (1996): 353–90.

———. "How Liability Law Affects Medical Productivity." *Journal of Health Economics* 21 (2002): 931–955.

King, N. J. "Postconviction Review of Jury Discrimination: Measuring the Effect of Juror Race on Jury Decisions." *Michigan Law Review* 92 (1993): 63–130.

Kornhauser, L. A. and R. L. Revesz. "Multidefendant Settlements: The Impact of Joint and Several Liability." *Journal of Legal Studies* 23(1:1) (1994): 41–76.

Krauss, Michael I. "Restoring the Boundary: Tort Law and the Right to Contract." Cato Policy Analysis No. 347, Washington, D.C.: Cato Institute, 1999.

Kritzer, Herbert M. "Seven Dogged Myths Concerning Contingency Fees." *Washington University Law Quarterly* 80 (2002): 739–784.

———. "The Wages of Risk: The Returns of Contingent Fee Legal Practice." *DePaul Law Review* 47 (1998): 275.

Landes, Elisabeth M. "Insurance, Liability, and Accidents: A Theoretical and Empirical Investigation of the Effect of No-Fault Accidents." *Journal of Law and Economics* 25(1) (1982): 49–65.

Langley, Monica. "Bayer Pressed to Settle a Flood of Suits Over Drug, Fights Back." *Wall Street Journal* May 3, 2004.

Lempert, R. "Civil Juries and Complex Cases." In *Verdict: Assessing the Civil Justice System*, ed. R. E. Litan, 181–247. Washington, D.C.: Brookings Institution, 1993.

Levy, Robert. "Hired Guns Corral Contingent Fee Bonanza." *Legal Times.* February 1999.

Lieberman, J. K. *The Evolving Constitution.* New York: Random House, 1992.

Litan, Robert E. "The Safety and Innovation Effects of U.S. Liability Law: The Evidence." *American Economic Review* 81(2) (1991): 59–64.

———. *Verdict: Assessing the Civil Jury System*, Washington, D.C.: Brookings Institution, 1993.

Loughran, David S. *The Effect of No-Fault Automobile Insurance on Driver Behavior and Automobile Accidents in the United States* Santa Monica, Calif.: RAND Institute for Civil Justice, 2001.

MacKinnon, F. B. *Contingency Fees for Legal Services*. Chicago: American Bar Association, 1964.

Maloney, Michael T., Robert E. McCormick, and Robert D. Tollison. "Economic Regulation, Competitive Governments, and Specialized Resources." *Journal of Law and Economics* 27 (1984): 329–338.

Manning, Richard L. "Changing Rules in Tort Law and the Market for Childhood Vaccines." *Journal of Law and Economics* 37(1) (1994): 247–275.

Manski, C. F. and S. R. Lerman. "The Estimation of Choice Probabilities from Choice-Based Samples." *Econometrica* 45 (1977): 1977–1988.

Marder, N. "The Interplay of Race and False Claims of Jury Nullification." *University of Michigan Journal of Legal Reform* 32 (1999): 285–321.

Martin, Robert. "General Aviation Manufacturing: An Industry under Siege." *The Liability Maze: The Impact of Liability Law on Safety and Innovation*. Washington, D.C.: Brookings Institution 1991.

McClellan, F. M. "The Dark Side of Tort Reform: Searching for Racial Justice." *Rutgers Law Review* 48 (1996): 761–798.

McClellan, M. B. "Merit Appointment versus Popular Election: A Reformer's Guide to Judicial Selection Methods in Florida." *Florida Law Review* 43 (1991): 529–560.

Miller, Geoffrey P. "Some Agency Problems in Settlement." *Journal of Legal Studies* 16 (1987): 189–215.

Miller, Neal. "An Empirical Study of Forum Choices in Removal Cases Under Diversity and Federal Question Jurisdiction." *American University Law Review* 41(369) (1992): 369–452.

Milliman USA. *Understanding Health Plan Administrative Costs*. 2003.

Neely, R. *The Product Liability Mess*. New York: The Free Press, 1988.

Nicholson, M. A. and N. Nicholson. "Funding Judicial Campaigns in Illinois." *Judicature* 77(6) (1994): 294–299.

Olson, Walter. *The Litigation Explosion*. New York: Truman Talley Books, 1991.

———. "Sue City: The Case Against the Contingency Fee." *Policy Review* Winter 1991, http://walterolson.com/articles/contingcy1.html (accessed on March 22, 2005).

Polinksy, A. M. and D. L. Rubinfeld. "A Note on Settlements Under the Contingent Fee Method of Compensating Lawyers." *International Review of law and Economics* 22 (2002): 217–225.

Posner, R. A. "An Economic Approach to Legal Procedure and Judicial Administration." *Journal of Legal Studies* 2 (1973): 399–459.

———. *The Federal Courts: Challenge and Reform*. Cambridge, Mass.: Harvard University Press, 1996.

———. "What Do Judges Maximize? (The Same Thing Everybody Else Does)." *Supreme Court Economic Review* 4 (1993): 1–41.

Pear, Robert. "Mississippi Gaining as Lawsuit Mecca." *The New York Times,* August 20, 2001.

Priest, George L. "Can Absolute Manufacturer Liability Be Defended?" *Yale Journal on Regulation* 9(1), (1992): 237–263.

———. "The Current Insurance Crisis and Modern Tort Law." *Yale Law Journal* 96(7) (1987): 1521–1590.

———. "Introduction: The Problem and Efforts to Understand It. in C. R. Sunstein, R. Hastie, J. W. Payne, D. A. Schkade and W. K. Viscusi, eds., *Punitive Damages: How Juries Decide.* Chicago: University of Chicago Press, 2002.

———. "The Modern Expansion of Tort Liability: Its Sources, Its Effects, and Its Reform." *Journal of Economic Perspectives* 5(3) (1991): 31–50.

———. *Public Citizen Litigation Group Quarterly Update,* July 28, 2000, http://www.citizen.org/litigation/about/articles.cfm?ID=554 (last accessed June 20, 2005).

Priest, George L. and B. Klein. "The Selection of Disputes for Litigation." *Journal of Legal Studies* 13(1) (1984): 1–55.

Putnam, William Lowell. *John Peter Zenger and the Fundamental Freedom.* McFarland & Company, 1997.

RAND Corp., Allan Abrahamse, Scott Ashwood, Stephen J. Carroll Deborah Hensler, Jennifer Gross, Elizaebeth Sloss, and Michelle White. *Asbestos Litigation Costs and Compensation: An Interim Report.* Santa Monica, Calif.: RAND Corp. 2002.

Rickman, Neil. "Contingency Fees and Litigation Settlement." *International Review of Law and Economics* 19 (1999): 295–317.

Rosen, J. "Jurymandering." *The New Republic* November 30, 1992, 15.

Rowland, C. K. and R. A. Carp. *Politics and Judgment in Federal District Courts.* Lawrence, Kansas: University Press of Kansas, 1996.

Rubin, Paul H. *Tort Reform by Contract.* Washington, D.C.: American Enterprise Institute, 1993.

Rubin, Paul H. and Shepherd, Joanna, "Tort Reform and Accidental Deaths" (August 10, 2005). *Emory Law and Economics Research Paper* No. 05-17 http://ssrn.com/abstract=781424.

Rubinfeld, Daniel and Suzanne Scotchmer. "Contingency Fees for Attorneys: An Economic Analysis." *RAND Journal of Economics* 24 (1993): 343–357.

———. "Contingency Fees". In Peter Newman, ed. *New Palgrave Dictionary of Economics and the Law.* New York: MacMillian Press, 1998.

Schroeder, Christopher. "The Multistate Settlement Agreement and the Problem of Social Regulation Beyond the Power of State Government." *Seton Hall Law Review* 31 (2001): 612–616.

Schuck, P. H. "Mapping the Debate on Jury Reform." In *Verdict: Assessing the Civil Jury System,* ed. R. E. Litan, 306–40. Washington, D.C.: Brookings Institution, 1993.

Schwartz, Murray L. and Daniel J. B. Mitchell. "An Economics Analysis of the

Contingency Fee in Personal-Injury Litigation." *Stanford Law Review* 22 (1970): 1125–1162.

Seabury, Seth, Nicholas Pace, and Robert Reville. 2004. Forty Years of Civil Jury Verdicts. *Journal of Empirical Legal Studies* 1(1):1–25.

Seltzer, R., J. M. Copacino, and D. R. Donahoe. "Fair Cross Section Challenges in Maryland: An Analysis and Proposal." *University of Baltimore Law Review* 35 (1996): 127–167.

Silverman, B. W. *Density Estimation for Statistics and Data Analysis.* London: Chapman and Hall, 1986.

Smith, Janet K. and Steven R. Cox. "The Pricing of Legal Services: A Contractual Solution to the Problem of Bilateral Opportunism." *Journal of Legal Studies* 14 (1958): 167–183.

Social Security Administration. *SSA's Performance and Accountability Report for Fiscal Year 2003.* Social Security Administration [Available at http://www.ssa.gov /policy/docs/statcomps/di_asr/2002/index.html] 2003.

Stiglitz, Joseph, Jonathan Orszag, and Peter Orszag. "The Impact of Asbestos Liabilities on Workers in Bankrupt Firms." *Journal of Bankruptcy Law and Practice* 12 (2003): 51–92.

Stine, R. A. "Data Analysis Using Mathematica." In *Computational Economics and Finance*, ed. H. R. Varian, pp. 330–361. New York: Telos, 1996.

Studdert, David and Troyen Brennan. "Beyond Dead Reckoning: Measures of Medical Injury Burden, Malpractice Litigation, and Alternative Compensation Models From Utah and Colorado." *Indiana Law Review* 33 (2000): 1643–1686.

Stumpf, H. P. and J. H. Culver. *The Politics of State Courts.* New York: Longman, 1992.

Tabarrok, Alexander and Eric Helland. "Court Politics: The Political Economy of Tort Awards." *Journal of Law and Economics* 42 (1999): 157–188.

———. 1999. Court Politics: The Political Economy of Tort Awards. *Journal of Law and Economics* XLII,1 (April): 157–188.

Thomas, Ralph and Andrew Garber. "Out-of-State Donors Feed Gregoire Fund." *Seattle Times* October 28, 2004, http://seattletimes.nwsource.com/html/localnews /2002074950_gregoire28m.html (accessed June 2, 2005).

Thomason, Terry. "Are Attorneys Paid What They're Worth? Contingency Fees and the Settlement Process." *Journal of Legal Studies* 20 (2004): 218.

Tillinghast-Towers Perrin. *U.S. Tort Costs: 2000 Update. Trends and Findings on the Costs of the U.S. Tort System.* 2000.

———. *U.S. Tort Costs: 2003 Update. Trends and Findings on the Costs of the U.S. Tort System.* 2003.

Tullock, Gordon. 1998. Juries. In *The New Palgrave Dictionary of Economics and the Law*, vol 2. ed. Peter Newman (London: Macmillan), pp. 395–400. Reprinted in Volume 1 of the *Selected Works of Gordon Tullock*, Charles Rowley (ed). Liberty Fund, Indianapolis, 2004.

U.S. Congress. *Class Action Fairness Act of 2005*, 109th Cong., 1st sess. (February 18, 2005). Public Law 109–202.U.S. Congress. Senate. "Class Action Fairness Act of 2003." 108th Congress. 2003. s 1751

U.S. Department of Justice. *Civil Jury Cases and Verdicts in Large Counties*. Washington, DC: Bureau of Justice Statistics, www.ojp.usdoj.gov/bjs/, 1995.

——. *Civil Jury Cases and Verdicts in Large Counties, 1996*. Washington, DC: Bureau of Justice Statistics, www.ojp.usdoj.gov/bjs/, 1999.

Vidmar, Neil. *Medical Malpractice and the American Jury*. Ann Arbor: University of Michigan Press, 1997.

Viscusi, W. Kip. "The Challenge of Punitive Damages Mathematics." *Journal of Legal Studies* 30(2:1) (2001): 313–350.

——. "The Determinants of the Disposition of Product Liability Claims and Compensation for Bodily Injury." *Journal of Legal Studies* 15 (1986): 321–346.

——. "Product and Occupational Liability." *Journal of Economic Perspectives* 5(3) (1991): 71–91.

——. *Smoke-Filled Rooms: A Postmortem on the Tobacco Deal*. Chicago: University of Chicago Press, 2002.

——. "Why There Is No Defense of Punitive Damages." *Georgetown Law Journal* 87(2) (1998): 381–394.

Viscusi, W. Kip and Michael J. Moore. "Rationalizing the Relationship between Product Liability and Innovation." *Tort Law and the Public Interest: Competition, Iinnovation, and Consumer Welfare*. New York and London: W. W. Norton. 1991.

——. "Product Liability, Research and Development, and Innovation." *Journal of Political Economy* 101(1) (1993): 161–84.

Waehrer, Geetha M. and Ted R. Miller. "Restricted Work, Workers' Compensation, and Days Away from Work." *Journal of Human Resources* 38(4) (2003): 964–991.

Waldfogel, J. "The Selection Hypothesis and the Relationship Between Trial and Plaintiff Victory." *Journal of Political Economy* 103(2) (1995): 229–260.

White, Michelle. "Explaining the Flood of Asbestos Litigation: Consolidation, Bifurcation, and Bouquet Trials." (*National Bureau of Economic Research Working Paper 9362*, 2002)

Willging, Thomas E., Laural L. Hooper, and Robert J. Niemic. *Empirical Study of Class Actions in Four Federal District Courts: Final Report to the Advisory Committee on Civil Rights*. Federal Judicial Center, 1996.

Wright, C. A. *Law of Federal Courts*. 5th ed. St. Paul, Minn..: West Publishing Co., 1994.

Zywicki, Todd J. "The Economics of Credit Cards." *Chapman Law Review* 3 (2000): 166–170.

Index

NOTE: In this index, *notes* are indicated by an "*n*," *tables* are indicated by a "*t*," and *figures* are indicated by an "*f*" following the page number.

A

administrative costs of tort system and alternatives, 11–15, 14*t*

Administrative Office of the U.S. Courts, 3, 25

See also Federal data

Alabama as "tort hell," 21

American Jury, The (Kalven and Zeisel), 50–51

American Tort Reform Association (ATRA), 141*n*13

analysis. *See* regression results

appointment judicial selection system, 68–69, 108*t*, 142*n*1

Aspin, L. T., 142*n*1

asymptotic standard errors, 66*t*

ATRA (American Tort Reform Association), 141*n*13

attorneys. *See* lawyers

Auto as case-type variable, 32*t*, 33*f*, 37, 55*t*, 60*t*, 62*t*, 64–66*t*, 76*t*, 82*t*, 89*t*, 110*t*, 121*t*

automobile-injury cases

as case-type variable, 37–38

data on, 32*t*

automobile-injury cases (*cont.*)

regression of log awards in jury trials, 54, 55

time to trial results for, 66*t*

See also injuries

Avery v. State Farm Mutual Auto Insurance, 127

Award for Jury and Judge regression results, 59–61, 60*t*

Award on Jury Trials regression results, 52, 54–57, 55*t*

Awards Decline in Poverty Rates at Low Poverty Rates but Increase Rapidly at Higher Rates, 43–44, 44*f*

Awards on Race and Poverty Variables regression results, 32*t*, 34–37, 34*t*

B

Bad Faith as case-type variable, 37–38, 55*t*, 56, 60*t*, 64*t*, 79, 82*t*, 89*t*

bad faith cases, 57, 79

Bernstein, David, 49–50, 63, 114, 122, 140*n*2

Bifurcated Trial as variable, 80, 83*t*

Black as variable, 34*t*, 35, 39*t*, 43*t*, 45*t*

black lung benefits, 14*t*, 136*n*7

Black Lung Disability Trust Fund, 136*n*7

black poverty rate

award correlation, 34*t*, 39–41, 39*t*, 43–44, 43*t*, 44*f*

black poverty rate (*cont.*)
  Black as variable, 34*t*, 35, 39*t*, 43*t*, 45*t*
  formula for, 32, 34–37, 34*t*
  overview, 46–47
  and win rates, 46
Blue Cross-Blue Shield administrative
  costs, 13
Bonfire of the Vanities, The (Wolfe), 1
Brickman, Lester, 115, 117–19, 121, 144*n*2
"Bronx effect," 1

C
CAFA (Class Action Fairness Act),
  128–29
campaign contributions, 72–74, 92,
  142–43*n*6
caps on awards
  economic, 55*t*
  non-economic, 55*t*, 56, 57–58, 60, 64*t*,
    80, 82, 89–90*t*
  pain and suffering, 57–58
  punitive, 55*t*, 56–57, 60, 64*t*, 80,
    82–83, 89–90*t*
caps on contingent fees, 21, 96–98,
  102–4, 105–10, 108–9*t*, 110*t*, 124
Carbon, S. B., 142*n*1
case categories
  bad faith cases, 37–38, 55*t*, 56, 57, 60*t*,
    64*t*, 79, 82*t*, 89*t*
  controlling for differences in awards
    based on, 52, 54
  employment, 37–38
  in judge sample, 54
  variables in regression analysis,
    37–38, 142*n*17
  wrongful termination, 37, 56, 79, 80,
    141*n*11
  See also injuries; medical-malpractice
    cases; premises-liability cases;
    product-liability cases
case screening through contingent fees,
  101–4

cause-based compensation systems, 12,
  14*t*
Civil Justice Survey of State Courts (U.S.
  Department of Justice), 24–25,
  106–7, 121
  See also State Courts data
Class Action Fairness Act (CAFA),
  128–29
class-action lawsuits, 1, 95, 97–98,
  127–28, 142*n*8
Clermont, Kevin M., 51, 142*n*5
Collateral Sources as variable, 55*t*, 60*t*,
  64*t*, 80, 82*t*, 83, 89*t*
collateral sources rule
  diversity jurisdiction regressions, 89*t*
  effect of weakening, 80
  and judges, 59, 60*t*, 64*t*
  in jury trials, 55*t*, 57, 59
  state regression results, 82*t*, 83, 89
COMP database, 75
Compensation for Injury, Illness, and
  Fatality in the United States (2001),
  12–15, 14*t*
compensation systems, 11–12
conditional fees, 99–100, 105
Contingent Fee Limits by State in
  Medical Malpractice, Personal
  Injury, and Workers' Compensation
  Cases, 96, 107–9, 108–9*t*
contingent fees
  for doctors, 101, 145*n*11
  economic fundamentals, 98–102
  versus hourly fees, 101–3, 106–7, 110*t*,
    111–12, 114–19, 122, 124, 144*n*2
  hypothesis, 124
  lawyers returns with, 115–19
  limits on, 21, 96–98, 102–4, 105–10,
    108–9*t*, 110*t*, 124
  and non-US legal systems, 145*n*t
  regression analysis, no limits, 62*t*, 65*t*
  as screening device, 102–4
  and settlements, 110–15

variation, sources of
  county poverty rates, 26, 35–36, 47,
    139*n*22, 140*n*23
  judge and jury samples, 54–55, 58
venture capitalists of torts, 100
Viscusi, Kip, 20, 137*n*4

W
wage effect on tort awards, 36
Weak Joint and Several Liability as
  variable, 80, 82*t*, 83, 89*t*
wealth redistribution, 1, 104
  See also partisan judicial election
    selection system
Wells, M. T., 137*n*4, 139*n*18
White as variable, 34*t*, 39*t*, 43*t*, 45*t*
white poverty rate
  and award correlation, 34*t*, 35–37,
    39–41, 39*t*, 43*t*, 46–47, 140*n*27
  and settlement correlation, 44–45, 45*t*
Win Decision: Jury versus Judge, 61, 62*t*
win rates
  by category of case, 75–76
  descriptive statistics for all variables,
    65*t*
  judge trials versus jury trials, 51–52,
    53*t*, 61–62, 62*t*
  and jury demographics, 137*n*5
  and poverty rates, 45–46
  and settlement rates, 46
Wolfe, Tom, 1
workers' compensation, 12–13, 14*t*
Wrice, Herman, 142*n*7
Wrongful Termination as variable, 37,
  56, 79, 80, 141*n*11

Z
Zeisel, Hans, 50–51, 141*n*5
Zenger trial, 125–26

About the Authors

Eric A. Helland is an associate professor of economics at Claremont McKenna College, senior economist at the RAND Corporation's Institute for Civil Justice, and a member of the plenary faculty at the Claremont Graduate School. During the 2002–03 term, Dr. Helland was a visiting fellow at the Stigler Center for the Study of the Economy and the State at the University of Chicago Graduate School of Business. In 2003–04, he served as a senior economist on the Council of Economic Advisers. Dr. Helland has been published in a wide variety of scholarly journals including the *Journal of Law and Economics*, the *Review of Economics and Statistics*, *Regulation*, and the *Journal of Environmental Economics and Management*.

Alexander T. Tabarrok is an associate professor of economics at George Mason University and Research Director for The Independent Institute. Scholarly articles by Dr. Tabarrok have appeared in the *Journal of Law and Economics*, *Public Choice*, *Journal of Health Economics*, *Journal of Theoretical Politics*, *Theory and Decision*, and many other journals. He is editor of The Independent Institute books *Entrepreneurial Economics: Bright Ideas from the Dismal Science* (Oxford University Press) and *Changing the Guard: Private Prisons and the Control of Crime* and co-editor (with D. Beito and P. Gordon) of *The Voluntary City* (University of Michigan Press). Dr. Tabarrok is also assistant editor of *The Independent Review*. Popular articles by Dr. Tabarrok have appeared in many magazines and newspapers.

INDEPENDENT STUDIES IN POLITICAL ECONOMY

THE ACADEMY IN CRISIS: The Political Economy of Higher Education | *Ed. by John W. Sommer*

AGAINST LEVIATHAN: Government Power and a Free Society | *Robert Higgs*

AGRICULTURE AND THE STATE: Market Processes and Bureaucracy | *E. C. Pasour, Jr.*

ALIENATION AND THE SOVIET ECONOMY: The Collapse of the Socialist Era | *Paul Craig Roberts*

AMERICAN HEALTH CARE: Government, Market Processes and the Public Interest | *Ed. by Roger D. Feldman*

ANTITRUST AND MONOPOLY: Anatomy of a Policy Failure | *D. T. Armentano*

ARMS, POLITICS, AND THE ECONOMY: Historical and Contemporary Perspectives | *Ed. by Robert Higgs*

BEYOND POLITICS: Markets, Welfare and the Failure of Bureaucracy | *William C. Mitchell & Randy T. Simmons*

THE CAPITALIST REVOLUTION IN LATIN AMERICA | *Paul Craig Roberts & Karen LaFollette Araujo*

CHANGING THE GUARD: Private Prisons and the Control of Crime | *Ed. by Alexander Tabarrok*

THE CHE GUEVARA MYTH AND THE FUTURE OF LIBERTY | *Alvaro Vargas Llosa*

CUTTING GREEN TAPE: Toxic Pollutants, Environmental Regulation and the Law | *Ed. by Richard Stroup & Roger E. Meiners*

THE DIVERSITY MYTH: Multiculturalism and Political Intolerance on Campus | *David O. Sacks & Peter A. Thiel*

DRUG WAR CRIMES: The Consequences of Prohibition | *Jeffrey A. Miron*

THE EMPIRE HAS NO CLOTHES: U.S. Foreign Policy Exposed | *Ivan Eland*

ENTREPRENEURIAL ECONOMICS: Bright Ideas from the Dismal Science | *Ed. by Alexander Tabarrok*

FAULTY TOWERS: Tenure and the Structure of Higher Education | *Ryan C. Amacher & Roger E. Meiners*

FREEDOM, FEMINISM, AND THE STATE: An Overview of Individualist Feminism | *Ed. by Wendy McElroy*

HAZARDOUS TO OUR HEALTH?: FDA Regulation of Health Care Products | *Ed. by Robert Higgs*

HOT TALK, COLD SCIENCE: Global Warming's Unfinished Debate | *S. Fred Singer*

LIBERTY FOR WOMEN: Freedom and Feminism in the Twenty-First Century | *Ed. by Wendy McElroy*

MARKET FAILURE OR SUCCESS: The New Debate | *Ed. by Tyler Cowen & Eric Crampton*

MONEY AND THE NATION STATE: The Financial Revolution, Government and the World Monetary System | *Ed. by Kevin Dowd & Richard H. Timberlake, Jr.*

OUT OF WORK: Unemployment and Government in Twentieth-Century America | *Richard K. Vedder & Lowell E. Gallaway*

PLOWSHARES AND PORK BARRELS: The Political Economy of Agriculture | *E. C. Pasour, Jr. & Randal R. Rucker*

A POVERTY OF REASON: Sustainable Development and Economic Growth | *Wilfred Beckerman*

PRIVATE RIGHTS & PUBLIC ILLUSIONS | *Tibor R. Machan*

RECLAIMING THE AMERICAN REVOLUTION: The Kentucky & Virginia Resolutions and Their Legacy | *William J. Watkins, Jr.*

REGULATION AND THE REAGAN ERA: Politics, Bureaucracy and the Public Interest | *Ed. by Roger Meiners & Bruce Yandle*

RESTORING FREE SPEECH AND LIBERTY ON CAMPUS | *Donald A. Downs*

RESURGENCE OF THE WARFARE STATE: The Crisis Since 9/11 | *Robert Higgs*

RE-THINKING GREEN: Alternatives to Environmental Bureaucracy | *Ed. by Robert Higgs & Carl P. Close*

SCHOOL CHOICES: True and False | *John D. Merrifield*

STRANGE BREW: Alcohol and Government Monopoly | *Douglas Glen Whitman*

TAXING CHOICE: The Predatory Politics of Fiscal Discrimination | *Ed. by William F. Shughart, II*

TAXING ENERGY: Oil Severance Taxation and the Economy | *Robert Deacon, Stephen DeCanio, H. E. Frech, III, & M. Bruce Johnson*

THAT EVERY MAN BE ARMED: The Evolution of a Constitutional Right | *Stephen P. Halbrook*

TO SERVE AND PROTECT: Privatization and Community in Criminal Justice | *Bruce L. Benson*

THE VOLUNTARY CITY: Choice, Community and Civil Society | *Ed. by David T. Beito, Peter Gordon & Alexander Tabarrok*

WINNERS, LOSERS & MICROSOFT: Competition and Antitrust in High Technology | *Stan J. Liebowitz & Stephen E. Margolis*

WRITING OFF IDEAS: Taxation, Foundations, & Philanthropy in America | *Randall G. Holcombe*

For further information and a catalog of publications, please contact:

THE INDEPENDENT INSTITUTE
100 Swan Way, Oakland, California 94621-1428, U.S.A.
510-632-1366 · Fax 510-568-6040 · info@independent.org · www.independent.org